Journeys with Flies

Journeys with Flies

EDWIN N. WILMSEN

The University of Chicago Press

Chicago and London

Edwin Wilmsen is Research Fellow in Anthropology and visiting scholar at
the University of Texas at Austin. He is co-editor of *The Politics of Difference*
and the author of the award-winning book *Land Filled with Flies: A Political
Economy of the Kalahari.*

The University of Chicago Press, Chicago 60637
The University of Chicago Press, Ltd., London
© 1999 by The University of Chicago
All rights reserved. Published 1999

08 07 06 05 04 03 02 01 00 99   5 4 3 2 1
ISBN (cloth): 0-226-90018-5

Library of Congress Cataloging-in-Publication Data

Wilmsen, Edwin N.
        Journeys with flies / Edwin N. Wilmsen.
            p.   cm.
        Includes bibliographical references
        ISBN 0-226-90018-5 (alk. paper)
            1. Anthropology—Field work.   2. Anthropology—Philosophy.
        3. Wilmsen, Edwin N.   4. Anthropologists—United States—
        Biography.   I. Title.
        GN34.3.F53W55   1999
        301'.07'23—dc21   99-30469
                                                                                   CIP

⊗ The paper used in this publication meets the minimum requirements of
the American National Standard for Information Sciences—Permanence of
Paper for Printed Library Materials, ANSI Z39.48-1992.

For those who are in it

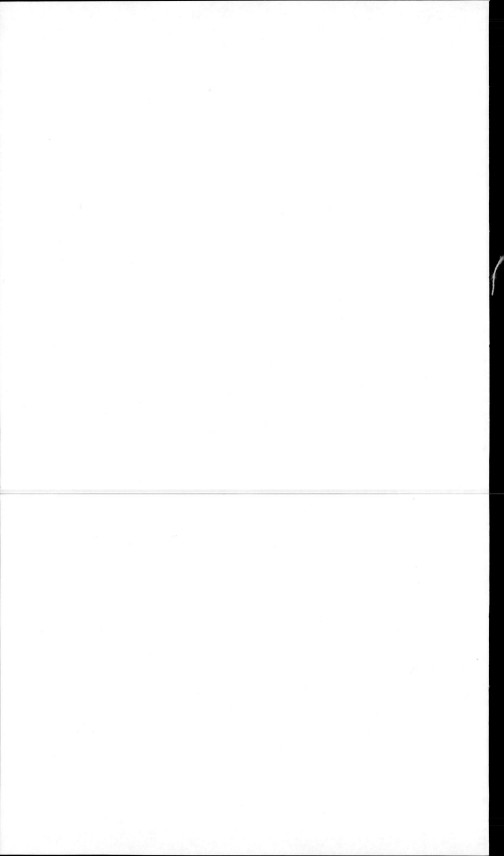

Contents

Geographies (on Kgali Hill)

Why is it,
here on this granite
Tswana rock,
that I think of Cape Cod
where I have never been —
and last year by Superior?

Is it the survey marker
black white
against pure sky blue?

Texas seacoast sands
once my domain
so long neglected;
Assateague I love —
Hatteras I have never seen
but dream of.

Tswana flies pestering me
seem as all that passed between
one idyll and another.

Prologue

I could say, as Malcolm Lowry perhaps said of his writing *Under the volcano:* . . . it's simpler than that; I wanted myself, in my own place, for a brief space. I'm sure I read this somewhere, but cannot remember where. It doesn't matter if it were true of Lowry or not; it is true of me. That simple motive is one of the reasons for this book.

But it's more complex, too. Ethnographies construct alien cultures. They cannot help but do so, for it is the role assigned to them by a western world which not too long ago set out across colonial waters to discover "the varieties of human experience." Many jewels have been unearthed in the search and displayed, often in settings of fine reporting. We are incomparably richer for this. The genuine advances Euroamerica has made in its evaluation of other peoples—however these advances may be debased, or even apparently lost, at times—have been fused by painstaking documentation of intrinsic value, inherent integrity, in other cultures. To exhibit the full scope of this integrity, ethnographers have polished the more esoteric facets of their finds. Like jewels, ethnographies are valued for the rarity of their contents. Reading them, varieties become exotics in the mind.

It can be argued that emphasis on the unfamiliar, the odd —perhaps, even the nonexistent—was part of a necessary, illuminating phase in the domestication of Euroamerican thought concerning the human condition. That could be true. But the ordinary in human experience is blinded by the light. And it is the ordinary that people share in their lives. The second motive for *Journeys* is set in my conviction that we have passed beyond the phase of esoterica and can now concentrate on the common. It seemed to me that a way to do this lay in exposing the simultaneity of experience in an individual life: recurrences in which earlier occurrences resonate — recognized as memories, expectations, reveries — informing each momentary awareness, shaping each.

Then: memory has a transitive quality. ⌐Separate lives are congruent in experience, no matter how disparate their cultural environments.⌐ Once the words are learned, native speakers of different languages begin to recognize each other — thirst thick under an arid sun, identical errors in navigating unknown landscapes, parallel blunderings through sexual awakening — in evoked images of their separate experiences. For it is individuals, not cultures, who meet and re-present their contexts to each other. The third motive for *Journeys* stems from this correlate of the second. I wanted to record these simultaneities as they are situated in my ethnographic setting, both that part in which I am native and that in which I will always remain neophyte, erasing thereby the exotic in either.

Journeys has had a long genesis.[1] I had been in CaeCae about three weeks in 1973 when Zona — an older, highly respected, somewhat feared man — agreed to allow me to accompany him to his snare lines. We could say very little to each other: I had some vocabulary of Zhu, Mbanderu, and Tswana nouns — mainly names of animals and plants (I had bought along field guides to the mammals, birds, and plants of Africa and in endless sessions of pointing to pictures had learned more than a hundred by then) — but few verbs, and only a rudimentary grasp of Zhu grammar, none of Mbanderu and Tswana. While walking in the debilitating heat, I asked myself how I was going to make my experience intelligible to others.

In the ensuing years I have enlarged that question. A central problem for anthropology has always been how to transform observation into presentation. Recognition of this problem has an ancient pedigree in the profession, going back to its beginnings. To transform what one knows — even of what is genuinely false or purely fiction or simply fabricated — into something knowable by others entails this inescapable tension between experience and presentation. A tension that must, of course, be resolved by anyone who constructs a text, not only by anthropologists. In ethnography, however, not only must a text be contextualized in the author's experience, but that experience must itself be contextualized in the setting for which there are no other witnesses.[2] And for anthropologists, as for others, the partitioning of reality is frequently no more than fiat, the endproduct of a process that too often compartmentalizes knowledge into objects thereby reducing subjective experience to a mere objective appendage. The continuous dialectical transformation of subject and object is lost in this process.

Shula Marks has struck just the right note:

> Historians should be able to write in chords, for our very medium distorts our intentions by its linear imperatives. We can only say one thing at a time, so that our ordering . . . is necessarily arbitrary and a poor reflection of the rich texture of historical experience.[3]

And in counterpoint, David Byrne:

> I guess the thing is that most of the time you get a sense from strict narrative that there's only one thing going on, and in today's world people are more used to bouncing from one thing to another and experiencing different things simultaneously.[4]

Journeys was written between 1977 and 1982.[5] Except for a very few additions where noted (or where dates make it obvious), all the sections were composed in the interstices of the events described—while driving or walking, during conversations and such—and written down at the first opportunity. This prologue, originally a much longer epilogue, was written in 1982–83, when I assembled some parts of the text for a failed attempt at publication.[6] Other exigencies, especially the writing of *Land filled with flies*, then demanded priority and the original manuscript of *Journeys* plus fragments not included in the first assemblage (but interpolated into the present piece) were set aside for a dozen years. In the interim a great deal has been written about intersubjectivity, authorial authority, and the subjunctive nature

of knowledge. As well, ethnographic writing has changed; esoterica are more rarely now the most valued facets of societies. I
was tempted, briefly, to engage the relevant literatures here, but
that would have made the text didactic and given it a false scho-
lastic context.

I have tried only to translate the texture of experience without claiming it to be mine alone, to capture chords in words. I
wanted to render my experience in ways that could resonate
with those of my readers. Simultaneously, I wanted to render
what I know of the experience of my African colleagues in ways
that could sound their resonance with mine, and through this
open the way for those who have not been there to recognize the
commonalty among us all. At the same time—redundantly, perhaps, but purposefully, since redundancy can remove all room
for doubt—I wanted to demonstrate that simultaneity of experience is not an exclusive prerogative of today's world but is a
condition of being human.

I wanted to find a way to express the historicities of persons
in contact—to express the fact that there are no alien cultures,
only alienating ways of categorizing diversity.

A brief map to the text is in order. More than a dozen peoples of
different language groups live in the Kalahari; I have been most
closely involved with three. One is a Khoisan-speaking group
who call themselves Zhutoasi (zhu = people; toa = completed or
finished; si = plural; therefore their name for themselves means
completed people). "Zhu" is my simplified abbreviation of this
name.[7] In the anthropological literature, these people have often
been designated !Kung. They have also been called Bushmen, a
term with derogatory connotations equivalent to nigger, which
I employ only in satire of colonial contexts—whether past or
present. The other people with whom I have been associated are
Bantu-speaking: Ovambanderu and Batswana, the first are pri-
marily cattle keepers, the latter agriculturalists who also keep
many cattle.

In the mythology of the region, god eats flies. It is not the creator (analogous to the Creator in Genesis but more closely identified with Jesus, and honey and bees) but rather the administrator of the world (one could think of Satan) who eats flies and attracts them to himself in his home in the sky by smearing shit around his mouth. But he does this only when he causes too few people to die, for humans are the first food of the gods. This is the rationale for human death which would otherwise be irrational, because people—unlike animals—are not proper food for beings on earth. For these inversions of sensible behavior and others, Zhu say "Gqanwa kwarra ncin"—god (the administrator) has no sense. He is, thus, a figure of ridicule as well as of fear and respect.

During hot dry months when the taste of food is all but forgotten in the Kalahari, flower-hued butterflies flock to fresh cowpies from which to syphon the only liquid available to them. During hot rain months when food is abundant, one need not be a shit-faced god to attract flies of many species in uncountable numbers which all on their own are a constant irritant as they suck sweat from skin and tears from eyes of humans and animals alike; some bite or sting painfully. Flies, thus, became for me a metaphor of the contradictions and ambiguities in life. This metaphor formed the title of my political economy of the Kalahari, *Land filled with flies,* where it is used in tropic irony, transferring the symbol to colonial and neocolonial administrators and their distortions of the social realities of the region, and further to that particular form of ethnographic practice which perpetuates those distortions. In *Journeys,* the metaphor is reduplicated: not only are there contradictions and ambiguities in life but also in subjunctive encounters with lives.

Journeys with Flies

The passenger does not see the same rigging as the sailors.
Jorge Luis Borges, *The book of sand*

The world has a way of looking at people
sometimes it seems that the world is wrong.
Talking Heads, *The great curve*

The sundering of a scientific from a poetic truth is the primal mark
of the administrative mind.
Russell Jacoby, *Social amnesia*

Beginnings

Persimmons tasted first in stories brought to me from China
were taken back in nightmares, those lines drawn between
dreams . . .

fear that the quarter saved from nickels left under pillows by
tooth-fairies, pennies paid for carpets hung over clotheslines and
beaten on Saturdays to buy my first real red persimmon, as costly
as a boy's shirt at that time, would be taken by some phantom
neighbor bully while my faithful white dog stood by. Faithfully,
another dream stayed with me while awake: the searching space
inside a mother's eyes asking why the wind blew only broken
crates and tar across a driven sea.

> Release me from that dream; release
> me from the smell of cracked
> kitchen paint washed each spring in
> preparation for a new coat of
> smudge borne by sea air.
> You taught me to use ashes for cleanser.
>> What other secrets did you
>> take with you?
> What secret wound cut into those
> eyes as I ran, so far away from
> paint and ashes? So far from that
> other dream, never to be awakened,
> where we talked of eating
> persimmons in a place you lived,

not here.

Here,
I continue on the skin of countries,
looking for the place that will bury me without a trace,
ephemeral as scars scratched by wind on the sea,
as if to readmit as rain the blood torn from shoulders
thirsting for a lover's nails

that close too soon . . .

>   I did not want to hurt you.
>   I clung so, not to leave you,
>   but to draw you down within me
>   where I did not want to go alone,
>
>   where I could not take you.

Yet, on my way — trying, now, to remember those eyes,
forgetting how to make the paint stay white and dry;
I heard the wind stop
and the sea cease to be an answer. Still,

leaving a scent of uneaten persimmons descending to Johannesburg the jumbo jet slides down the mountain slope; enormous
Magaliesberg boulders piled together, a litter clothed in sparse
fuzz of vegetation, kittens or puppies   —   perhaps.

Air thick with heavy palette of dryland sunset.

First attempts at reality are unsuccessful;
those are elephants piled together, not
kittens. Shadows of the rocks themselves,
slipping over bulging flanks, bring the mass to life.
Snuggling together for the comfort of contact.

My comfort.

Before I have seen an African animal in its own place, before I
have heard a hyaena laugh or a jackal cry, the fantasy landscape is

painted for me by Tutuola and Achebe rather than the brothers Grimm. Dead branches, fallen trees distill the unknowns of Kalahari nights into an indigenous grotesque existence, foreign to me; preconceived, but unfamiliar.

Six years later: forced by a broken axle to sleep alone in the bush—listening vaguely to lions purring beyond the firelight, knowing I am as safe here, enveloped in the flame-thrown hemisphere, as in the belly of the most modern airplane,[8] no longer needing conscious awareness of desert details now registered automatically without disturbing thoughts—things that began for me long ago, or recently, some that may begin in a possible future, mix in my mind, creating a new reality—or fantasy:

a glowing log, fire-tongue stabbing the empty air, becomes a basilisk.

The unknowns are again of a familiar kind.

To navigate that circle beginning in a distillation of place and time and history called Texas, through CaeCae seemingly at so many opposite poles of place and time and history, arriving at a transitory port of resolution having discovered that the poles are not opposites but are reference points marking the one truth about the future: that it is empty and will be filled for the most part with what we already know to be wrong, trying to reduce the wrong . . .

I had to measure dimensions:

> 12,983 kilometers / 9,179 air miles, New York– Johannesburg. My route was longer—through water wider in imagination than on maps—sea, Great Lakes; architecture; Arctic; archaeology; many more common points.

> 1,587 kilometers / 999 land miles, Johannesburg– CaeCae. In 1973, only the first part from Joburg paved

through replicas of Panhandle farming towns westward to Zeerust, 109 km; then north to Gaborone, 123 km across the low flank of the Dwarsberge, the rock-littered road beat brains bones tires to a homogeneous mess; 453 unpaved, seldom-graded kilometers to Francistown could be done in a long day. From there to Maun a Rhodesian zoologist called the road a 300-mile nightmare of sand, but it wasn't uniformly that bad and sometimes the Makgadikgadi Pans through which the road passes are flooded. At the bottom of the Kalahari, these huge salt and alkaline flats, normally dry, evaporate the final run-off from Angolan rainfall six months after it saturates the forest. And then there can be a lot of water—19 continuous kilometers in January 1974 to go through gaps between trees marking the supposed route; at Nata, a third of the way from Francistown, there is petrol pumped by hand, after that only cattle zebra wildebeest on the road. In Maun, a postbox where letters wait for me, trader's stores, hot showers. Much of the rest of the way is uninhabited track. In 1973, there were only 40 km of pavement in Botswana, all in the three European inspired towns; now, 1980: the road is paved as far as Nata and everyone drives faster than the 90kph speed limit, but still not a single traffic light in the country, only nineteen places to buy petrol.

222,000 mi^2 Botswana is about the size of Texas (262,134 mi^2) and 574,978 km^2 of France (549,619 km^2).

726,000 Batswana according to 1978 estimates, most of them along the edge of South Africa, the Republic not the subcontinent, strung out against the escarpment containing the Kalahari basin, along the line of rail begun by Rhodes to be a link in his Cape to Cairo scheme; not more than 2,000 of these people are Zhu—all in the northwest part of the country called Ngamiland, itself larger than New England minus Maine. 15,000 Mbanderu are clustered in a few locations around the country. CaeCae has six times as many Zhu as Mbanderu, only one Tswana man; about 250 in all.

900 meters/2,920 feet above sea level on the Makgadikgadi bottom, 1,090 meters/3,530 feet at CaeCae near the western edge of the country, average gradient less than a meter per mile. The Kalahari seems flat at first —but dunes undulate, fossil Pleistocene streambeds cut shallow troughs; a few eroded remnants of ancient rocks stick up in widely scattered places, such as Tsodilo. The landscape is more savannah than desert, covered with drought resistant grasses, deep-rooted woody shrubs, occasional trees—the land is bare only where overgrazed and around wells where waiting cattle goats donkeys horses churn the sand until they are watered.

43°C/110°F−45°C/115°F, actual Stevenson screen highs reached on some September–November afternoons, 40°C/104°F is common; 30°C/86°F seems cool in summer nights and almost hot as winter highs in June–July when the temperature may drop to −5°C/23°F for an hour or two toward the ends of really cold nights.

400 millimeters/16 inches of rain in an average year which seldom occurs; over 1,000 mm/40 in from October 1973 to May 1974; less than 175 mm/7 in during all of the years 1963–64; hardly ever a drop from May to October in any year. It isn't that there is so little rain (parts of the forested Yukon get no more), but that it evaporates so rapidly in the summer heat when it falls.

5:30 sunrise 7:30 sunset on 22 December's longest day; 7:30−5:30 on 21 June's austral winter solstice

—every day, many hours in the dark.

Uncountable illusions to overcome: the common schoolroom freight laid on to recruit Euroamerica into the first line of protection against any encroachment upon our leading role in civilization. Achebe has called these illusions the many evasions used to replace dialogue.[9]

Necessary to overcome the aridity of this "civilized" self-indulgence with its axiomatic assumption that other peoples exist to be made available to our understanding, that our understanding is the one that matters;[10] that they can only be made real, brought to life, by some Euram adventurer with a gift for turning words—almost by any zeal-driven missionary who feels moved to document supposed evidence in support of the myth, writing from the point of view that other peoples have a devastating lack of historical preparation, as if they had no history until we came along and showed them how.[11]

As necessary to overcome that aridity as to overcome the aridity of the desert: other dimensions . . .

> There are no beautiful days. The quality of a day, of a life, of a dream lies in our encounter with it, not in itself. Similarly, our understanding of another people lies not in themselves or in anything that they do but in our encounter with them. An encounter lived in experience crossed by qualification—partly in their world, and unavoidably in that segment of our world that surrounds us when we visit them. What we see of other peoples is shaped by this disjunction and in the expectations engendered by it. The view is invariably distorted. The essential anthropological project then is, or should be, to reduce the dimensions of this disjunction; the true anthropological moment occurs when us and them are recognized in the same terms, when observed and observer are not categorical opposites but are categorially equivalent agents in a unitary relation. That moment, if it has

ever been realized, has not yet been translated intelligibly to a larger audience. Our perceptions interfere with such presentation, and ethnographies are written from the perspective of a strictly outside observer, of a foreigner in the fullest sense of the term.

An instance: the belated, often reluctant, acknowledgement that peoples such as Zhu have a history as long as ours is too often immediately negated by the qualification that knowledge of those histories must remain shallow because their memories are short and they have no writing to remind them and we do not know how to excavate days and lives and dreams from sedimented human history. From that point it is an easy move to the notion that theirs are not histories in the same sense that we claim for ourselves: their histories are static without preparation for the present while ours are ever progressive into the future.[12]

Journeys started from this understanding and from the attendant understanding that my view of Zhu and Mbanderu is grounded differently from theirs. It became necessary to dig into the sediments in order to find the points where the rigging—seen differently by Borges's passenger and sailors—is anchored. Necessary to uncover the path of a past that brought me to my form of the present at CaeCae, while simultaneously finding their current present with its own past. It seemed to me that the conflict between subject and object dissolves at those points, the points where structure and history coalesce. Where passenger and sailor become one for a moment and see the same thing.

But seeing is not becoming; understanding is not being. I did not become one of them; to pretend to have done so—that it would be possible to do so—would be the final illusion.

19°50′S–21°05′E: CaeCae lies well within the tropics.

Entries

Thirsty. Thirsting skin flayed by sun and summer winds blown hot and dry in this desert. Sand driven into nerves ground raw.

A tiny shortbed Land Rover that looked like a worn-out toy: for seventy-five dollars its owner unloaded his cargo destined for a trader's store to make the 160 km side-trip westward to CaeCae where he left me under a tree in the dark, soon surrounded by people who made a fire for me and uttered not a single word that I recognized although they never stopped talking.

August: beginning of the hot season when accumulated wrongs — of the passed year, of the more distant past that had belonged to dead grandparents, spouse's relations — are added together in shouted rage, shored up sometimes by threats of bodily harm that one cannot be certain will not be inflicted . . .

A few weeks after my arrival:[13] two men, second cousins, at each others' throats:

> i'll put an arrow in him when he's out alone in the bush   he promised my mother two birds   she let him set snares around her dried-up cornfield   now he's eating all the birds he gets   now my mother is dying of hunger   there is no food
>
> i'll get him at night when he's asleep and no one sees   he made incestuous remarks to my wife   his father always did that to my mother who was his niece   saying things like i'll pull your long labia things like that you shouldn't say to people you can't marry   i don't get many birds[14]

Open threats, made public so they will not need to be acted upon; bound up tensions released . . .

Where the heat becomes too intense it must be vented upwards to escape in swirling pipes created by its own velocity into a sky cloudless for months.

In September, these dustdevils, like miniature tornados, rush through the thornbush every day, big ones with a rough grating roar, small ones with a sibilant swish; later, in October or November, two or three may be seen in a single field of vision with a thunderstorm pouring rain on another spot at the rate of an inch per hour.

At a distance, hidden behind the hump of a dune, their sound can mimic that of a truck engine

> a tow is coming[15]

followed by speculation that it is the sound of a Land Rover, or Toyota, Ford, or five-ton Bedford. But no vehicle appears.

Two weeks after I came to CaeCae: my first walk alone into the bush—not a courageous move, following the well-marked vehicle spoor leading eastward toward towns and stores and showerbaths. I had been delivered on this same road. Parting, my companions had said they would join me within two weeks, after their tenth-hand truck was repaired (an acquaintance had told us this vehicle was an unwise choice, but we knew he was not wise so ignored the valuable part of his experience); that time was now past, as it turned out another month would go by before I saw them again. While I learned through many repetitions to pronounce in Zhu a tow is coming, but not to distinguish a vehicle from the wind;

alternating between a desire to see my friends and being grateful for the chance to enter into this place free of their encumbrance . . .

There were three of us in the beginning, but in my memory I am alone.[16] We each had our own motives for coming to this remote corner of the Kalahari and our own interests couched in terms of scientific models and hypotheses of social behavior. The same co-ordinates described our location but the contours of the space that each of us entered were different even before we arrived in Botswana in July 1973. And, in fact, through a series of unplanned events that kept my companions at a distance, I was alone for the greater part of the next six months—as alone as one can be with 160 Zhu of all ages, more or less, and 35 Mbanderu, also com-ing and going, around the single set of open wells that held the only water for us all . . .

walking in this loose sand will take some learning; pushing off from toes only makes my foot slide backwards producing a lot of sweat but little forward motion . . .

> *no motion at all last year to the day exactly leaning into the wind trying to cross Arapahoe glacier and climb the peak with Carl and Lisa making no headway against the gale almost blown over when we turned to go back beginning then to make the plans that brought me here already telling them that if it worked out I wanted them to join me for a time realizing that more than a new language would have to be learned but not that ordinary things like walking would be different . . .*

Time to be bolder now, learn to navigate through the bush—more dense here than around the wells and camps where wood is cut for fences and firewood to open a space for cattle management and elimi-nate shelter for snakes. Can't see more than ten feet in any direction; shouldn't become irreparably lost, haven't come more than a mile al-though I've been gone an hour stopping to watch birds, study leaves, beginning to feel the texture of this landscape: cowpaths crisscross in all directions where cattle browse, easy to see they prefer acacias to broadleafs; follow the deep well-worn paths, they should take me back. Sitting on the tip of a twelve-foot termite hill everything looks the same, in every direction scraggly bushtops; the sun directly over-head projects no helpful shadows, wind still from the southwest so

this should be the way—unless the wind has shifted and that isn't
southwest . . .

> *hanging onto the leader of a jackpine trying to see over the uni-*
> *form tops of thousands of identical trees after a night snowstorm*
> *had obliterated all traces of trails . . .*

but there downhill is unquestionably the way to go,
here there are plenty of questions.

A few days later, far out in the bush with Twi, my namegiver-
grandfather, and Tjitjo and Damo, they ask where is CaeCae and
correct the point of my finger by three maybe five degrees laugh-
ingly saying I'll have to do better after I congratulate myself on
being so close—my turn will come three years later in Gaborone
when at the hotel I ask them to point to the center of town they
say we don't know this place; Damo perpetuates the joke in January 80 when again in Gaborone Ssao points in diametrically the
wrong direction to CaeCae and we recount stories of learning
local geographies.

I didn't particularly notice the young kid among the six or eight men
who settled around the fire next to my tent early every morning
to drink coffee before the sun was high and hot when we all moved
under the shade of a huge acacia tree of the kind called camelthorn
which Livingstone in his zeal though must have furnished the wood
for Noah's ark but really is most useful for dropping its big seed pods
eaten by cattle when grass is thin in order to first create and then
consolidate my beginning understanding of Zhu

In those days and for some time thereafter I would tell people I
spoke broken Bushman babytalk but felt secret satisfaction with
my babytalk when, ten weeks after arriving, I found myself one
night 40 km away with no companion other than Maitso, whom
I didn't know very well at the time, and was able to make myself
understood to total strangers.

but Damo was always there unobtrusive yet more often than not
lying closer rather than farther from me in the sand taking his turn

pronouncing a word or offering a construction running in response to the call "Daamuu" shouted by Katja or Maka the women of the Mbanderu family with whom his family had long been allied slipping back into his place when the errand was done laughing when Twi taught me to say I want you . . .

after a momentary flicker of embarrassment the three of us laughed too when I fell over soft unexpected forms on my way to pee out of the hemisphere of dancing cooking firelight in the third clouddark night of my Christmas party 75 as I sprawled with my head propped on my arm against Damo lying with Tabo still vivacious and desirable a young widow with two small kids she died a year later but at that moment I complimented their choice of a bed in the comparative seclusion of one of my shallow excavations into their recent history Damo telling me in those days that he would marry Ku but still had not worked out the end of his affair with Tabo while Ku clarified for me the particular kind of scoundrel he was since everybody knew that Damo would marry Ku and four years later have their third baby in her belly the first miscarried Kada nearly two now staying with his mother's older-sister in their father's camp to be weaned loving the cheese and candy we bring to him from our trips to Maun . . .

It seems impossible that six weeks after that first timid excursion I set out alone at dusk walking the eight kilometers to the hill camp to sleep there in order to leave before dawn on a kudu hunt with Kumsa having convinced him that my compass could guide me back should I become separated from him but not mentioning that in order to set a compass course the starting point must be known and because of that I won't bother to bring the compass next morning after several hours scanning we pick up fresh spoor and run along it closing the gap to a big male kudu which I never reach my glasses opaque with sweat tripped on a fallen tree I didn't see and watch Kumsa go on— then find my way back to his camp deserted at midday while everyone is out gathering food and on to CaeCae.[17]

No one is surprised . . .

I lost 4 kilos that day all water sweated out in the heat regained in
two hours drinking water and wine nearing home Mozart's 40th
floated to meet me and first I thought I had a heat high then that Polly
must have returned but it was Tjitjo playing her battery radio he said
I needed a bath

> get undressed   i'll heat water

poured in my "bathtub" lent by Manuel the kind of shallow enamelled
bowl I remember as a child seeing my sister bathed in England I think
they are called pudding basins after I had done all I could Tjitjo washed
my back . . .

I did need that bath although I preferred to wash no more than once
a week finding the accumulation of body-salt-oil-dirt less irritating
than the feeling of sweat-stuck sand forming immediately after a bath
and I did see the barrier of envy erected by a clean shirt changed
every day so I wore just one for a week too and later brought only
two with me we Tjitjo and I usually shared that one basin each week
with Damo John Ssao maybe a couple other men standing naked
around it in secluded bush near the wells scooping up water in cupped
hands washing each others backs.

At sixteen in 73, Tjitjo was already the tallest man in CaeCae; his face
physique personality commanding attention here as it would do any-
where. I can no longer imagine how he managed to make me understand that he intended to take charge of my camp or how I made him
understand the wage I could offer: some hand motions, sounds that
may have been words; the message carried between eyes looking
straight into each other, punctuated by "ee" repeated many times—
the Tswana word for "yes" the only sound we interpreted in common. He led me carefully by the hand through many intricacies of
local etiquette and knowledge . . .

literally as we quickly became confiding friends as men friends women
friends too hold hands here—in America of course I continue to be
inhibited about that just as at CaeCae I readily cut the forelimb from

a living animal while I still detest the mutilation of puppies' ears and tails under anesthesia in my own native land . . .

advising me to speak with women about their menstrual histories in groups to avoid sexual suggestions, working out strategies for estimating birthdates of people who have no calendar, teaching me to read enough Mbanderu to interpret his notes and to walk in the sand with side-slipping steps to disguise my spoor admitting that doing so didn't fool anyone simply allowed them the fiction of not knowing.

The last weeks of my stay in 1976 were hell tensions of impending departure expressed differently by different people: those who saw me as simply another transient begged for whatever I might leave behind; others tried to secure a hoard of tobacco against scarcity during my absence. Those close to me talked diverting trivia. Tjitjo and I quarreled often, insulted each other's intelligence manhood strength, sometimes silent for days—refused to bathe together; both feeling betrayed by circumstances and blaming the other.

We were peers in 1979 when I returned; he was secure as operator of the government-owned diesel-powered water pump installed two years previously (then the only steady wage job in the region) and with a beautiful modern trial wife his father had negotiated in Rakops, one of the vanguard among Mbanderu women changing to Western clothes—Kahai understood his son . . .

We talked as equals in the early morning and late night around his fire or mine about local politics, condition of cattle and markets for them, independence struggles in Namibia. Our houses open to each other as brothers. His duties now prevented him from making trips with me . . .

But on that day, returning from my first uncourageous walk into the bush, a horse is being saddled and a search party assembled; everyone certain I am lost.

*

By that time I had a name. Of course I knew about Zhu name relations, having read the literature that names give social dimension to biology of birth, that they construct the kinship universe
of persons named for grandparents and parents' siblings, thus
moulding the group together, specifying who may marry. But I
had no clue still have no satisfactory account of the negotiations
that led to Twi giving me his name and so becoming my grandfather, and it took a long time to learn who were my people and
what term to call them. If I'd had a choice I would not have selected Twi volatile angry too intelligent for the undereducated
role he is forced to play failing to find secure work with Whites
in Namibia forcing his kids to remain in a distant school thinking
they will find there the security he knows he can never have himself taking my things without asking saying you're my grandchild
what's yours is mine knowing as I did that this was not an extension of kin obligations but an extension of class the only way he
could exploit the exploiters . . .[18]

I don't know that one; you tell me.[19]

you want to be a Zhu   you have to learn footprints not just
     names

Uhn; it's a steenbok male.

duiker female

That one's a steenbok female.

young male

Female gemsbok with male calf.

uhn

November 73: walked with Tase to Twihaba to take an animal cen-
sus, sixty kay roundtrip; took no water, only one loaf of soda bread
—will rely on rainpools, and if we get no other food, milk from the
cattlepost established after rains began at Nwama. In the afternoon,
temperature well over 40°C, found a pool no more than a meter in

diameter, three or four centimeters deep, choked with reeds which we bent aside to find easily 100 thumb-sized fat frogs with bright green stripes and did not hesitate to drink half their home. Later, woke in the night to see a silent shape move in the moonless dark to lie under a bush twelve feet away, head resting on outstretched paws; chin on my hands crossed at blanket edge, we studied each other until imperceptibly I fell asleep and no longer saw her. In the morning I learned the sign of female leopard.

Returning, Tase tapped each spoor with his stick, its head a heavy burl-knob for use as a club, its end shaved sharp for digging:

> what's this one   today we'll be doing this all day   you should know them all by the time we get back to CaeCae

It took much longer. On our way, a hunting camp abandoned that morning by his uncle (knowing who it was by the footprints); cracking some of the scattered bones to eat the marrow—Tase had thrown his club at a bird, the only meat we had seen, but missed . . .

> *finding in an abandoned geology camp used in a premature hunt for oil on the Yukon coast in the 50s a rusted can of strawberry jam pulled open with our fingers scooping out the contents ravenous for sugar and fat our supply plane fogbound for weeks at Inuvik pilot biscuit and the caribou we shot thin in the calving season keeping us full but unsatisfied when the plane finally arrived we ate butter by the handful and had roaring diarrhea all that night that never lost the light of day . . .*[20]

At Nwama, Eiffel-rust rain etched across chalcedony-green afterlight sucked out of the mid-Atlantic where the rainbow arc of the sunken sun is gliding toward North America.

I can imagine that to be an organic reality, a function of the electrical charge of light clinging to its own perimeter and to reflections of important earth features—Guatemalan jungles could furnish the green for those bound to that place—wind carrying Eiffelcolor down with the shape blown into the rain. You can't be in only one place at a time—how could you find the way there, or ever return?

Coffee boiled for an hour in milk constantly skimmed so that it is like hot cocoa with a different taste, bitter roots roasted on a fire, and long after dark, the milking done, huge bowls of fresh clabbered yogurt . . .

all this milk. Just a month ago there was practically none; only cows with newly dropped calves had enough so that some could be taken for people to drink.

Those were hard days:

look at us

thinness is taking us

It was true. During the first sprinkles of the season—before rain had done anything other than raise hopes and freckle the sand —I went hunting with Zona; we returned with only a tortoise smaller than a fist and because it was hot and we had worked hard and I liked him and because he had been the first to allow me to accompany him hunting and today he had said I was a real Zhu when I saw the tortoise he overlooked, I gave him a cupful of mealie meal [21] to take to his older wife who was sick and had lost her appetite; the old man so happy he strutted around saying now we will eat jerking a leg up and cutting a sharp fart with each step, everyone rolling on the ground gasping he's been eating wild onions how can he say he's hungry. It was the last time he ever hunted. Old Sana, their first children more than forty years old, grew weaker while Zona spent all nights singing and dancing over her in an attempt to drive out the illness, succeeding only in exhausting himself.

The first time we hunted together, the first time I hunted here with anyone, Zona killed a steenbok and to show I would do my share, I carried it back to camp even though the cord binding its legs cut into my shoulder. Later, lying under the shade tree by his hut, Sana smoothing ostrich-eggshell beads against her thigh with a grindstone, the younger wife, Shea, putting what appeared to be old boards to bake in hot ashes while tending a boiling pot, everybody spitting into the sand from time to time and covering it with a flick of fingers; seeing myself in the droppings piling up under the donkey standing a few feet away because I suddenly remembered that my mother would sometimes illustrate what she meant about my being slow or lazy in learning something by telling me in German that the galloping donkey had left me behind, and thinking that the warm fertile smell that filled the air came out of those donkey droppings.

What are you putting into the ashes?

giraffe skin

Which was in fact as stiff and hard as a board hacked to pieces with an axe; and old, having been stored in the sun since it was killed not less than six months ago, but in roasting the hair burned off and the cells expanded and it became crackling just as hog skin does at home.

And in the pot?

stomach of yesterday's steenbok

And now I became really interested because even before I learned about galloping donkeys I liked trash meat as innards were called in Texas where I grew up . . .

> *my family called them that although we belonged to the class that either ate a lot of them or rationalized the absence of meat from the table by saying we don't like it all that much anyway we did have standards of course looked down on nextdoor neighbors who ate chicken feet fried in batter just like it was real meat after all you can go too far . . .*

Oh shit! Now I've gone too far; nothing could taste so awful. This stomach wasn't cooked in its contents exactly, those were dumped out, but a thick slime of semi-liquid semi-shit clung to it when it was thrown into the pot; that smell didn't come out of the donkey. Don't complain, there's more to lose than a little piece of rubbery shit; a big chunk of credibility could go down the tube. Shove it into a cheek pocket and practice the spitting, sand-flicking technique; talk about what we will do tomorrow.

Took a walk this evening—after writing twenty-five letters today in order to send them out with the game scout who passed through unexpectedly. Lovely sunset, air washed clear by last night's rain—saw the tawny eagle again, settling for the night; in the last light, eleven kudu—females with young—came out onto the molapo,²² played a few minutes, then ran at full tilt across to the south side, some jumping bushes taller than themselves, vanishing up the far ridge. Had been feeling low, result of writing all those letters, measuring the distance to people and things I miss. But the walk, the eagle, the evening, the kudu brought me around.

A hundred spoor counts, dozens of hunts, days upon days lying in the shades of trees learning who is related to whom, what is going into pots; a return to the States slipped between stays at CaeCae: on the short moving stair between concourses in Grand Central I have to navigate by myself for the first time—others have conveyed me here in planes, cabs, buses for pieces of paper, mutely exchanged for the most part—wrong currency or too few coins invariably offered, staring at greenback dollars as something foreign. Suddenly realizing that on this escalator I am confronted by more people than I have seen in nearly two years (thousands passed en route seen on the far sides of windows, mere specks in shifting landscapes); moving by rote rather than design.

In CaeCae, fewer people but missing anonymity.

A photograph of Heinrich Böll

The hut, begun a month ago, is almost finished. Wall and roof are complete except for a small section of thatch through which light still shows; it will be almost finished four months from now when rains begin in November or December, if they begin at all this year. I measured the hut this morning, on impulse: 2.2 meters in diameter. On one side, saddle, bridle, saddle blanket, knapsack, rope, other paraphernalia hang from forked branch-stubs allowed to protrude through the plaster; on the other hang clothes, bedroll, strips of dried eland meat, a couple of dressed birds, accumulating additions to my beadwork collection, pictures of people whose faces I want to see. Only half the floor is usable; the other half was patted into place yesterday: a plaster composed of fresh cowshit, sand, and water — the same material applied to lashed poles forms the round wall.

If the proportions are correct, more sand than shit, especially if termite-hill sand is used, a well-constructed hut will last ten years. Mine will not last so long. The first, built in 1973, was already crumbling and leaking when I left it in June 1976; only part of one wall is standing today.

It will be a week before the second half of this new floor will be dry. Even the usable half is still damp; on it are a footlocker full of books, a trunk filled with supplies, a small box of food, a sack of maize meal, two triple-width briefcases containing reference files and notebooks for recording data, blood collecting materials, a liquid nitrogen tank for storing sera, and an insulated box to protect film and cameras from the heat which will soon be oppressive, and the ever-present dust.[23]

The door has not yet been made. Winter night air flows into the hut, drawn in as warmth rises through the thatch; every morning there is an inch of ice on the water in the bucket outside. The fireplace, a slight circular depression to one side of the door opening, is too wet to use. Every night I must fold my foam pallet in half so it will fit the narrow strip of free floor beside the wet cowshit; the bed is then only a couple of centimeters wider than are my hips. Somehow it all seems spacious.

A paper edition of *Billiards at half-past nine* lies on the footlocker: Faehmel, an architect, plays billiards every morning, calculating trajectories—

> His memories had never been fixed in words and pictures, only in movements . . . Statics is the study of the equilibrium of forces, the study of conditions of tension and displacement in supporting structures; without statics you can't even build an African hut.[24]

A photograph of Heinrich Böll is reproduced on the cover of the book. Interruptions occur; the book is opened and closed. The photograph, set in motion, begins to speak as clearly as the written pages within. Böll's eyes are in the corners of their sockets looking to one side, past those things that are only measurable . . .

The room in Westgate is also small for four children.[25] The entire apartment is only twenty feet square, one of several in wooden World War II barracks floated up the Charles and converted to married student housing. I am studying architecture at MIT, candidate for the Master's degree. The year is 1959; Billiards has just been written. The room is exactly the length of two mattresses. Three years earlier I had built into it an L-shaped sleeping balcony; its short leg extends into the closet alcove in order to accommodate a third mattress across the width of the room. The clothes bar, lowered below balcony level to a height convenient for three to six year olds, is high enough nonetheless to allow the children's clothes to hang straight. Toy shelves and book shelves are fixed along the entire perimeter of the walls. The eldest, twins, cannot touch the balcony from the floor, which is free of obstacles except for those remaining after a day's play. The fourth bed just fits into a storage closet, a wall of which has been removed, opening it to the room; this bed is supported by a bureau bought at auction and cut in half, two drawers beside two drawers. Behind them, under the bed, is a cavern-like space entered through an opening left for the purpose between the drawer units. The children call this their Navaho hogan and bind up dolls in their new sister's cradleboard. Somehow, this room, too, seems spacious.

Reading to the children at bedtime, I sit on the floor: Aesop; Goethe, Reynard the fox; Le roman de roland; *Vachel Lindsey,* The Congo, Flower-fed buffalos; *Dylan Thomas; T. S. Eliot. Looking down from their beds, they often ask for Prufrock:*

> *I grow old . . . I grow old . . .*
> *I shall wear the bottoms of my trousers rolled,*
>
> *Shall I part my hair behind? Do I dare to eat a peach?*
> *I shall wear white flannel trousers, and walk upon the*
>   *beach.*
> *I have heard the mermaids singing, each to each.*
>
> *I do not think that they will sing to me.*[26]

They will sing to you, Daddy . . .

Often, when I hear them, I try to remember which of the children said that: They will sing to you.

First times

The time was indifferent to a ten year old boy sitting on the two-by-four rail of the wooden pavilion beside the lake at Kidd Springs Oak Cliff Dallas Texas watching sailors in summer whites with girls in cotton print dresses dance through warm nights in the second year of Our Second War To Make The World Safe For Democracy.

The white paint on the pavilion was peeling, revealing underlying streaks, also peeling, of that sick shade of turquoise that is one of the escutcheons of the U.S. Southwest — called aquamarine by neighbor ladies before Indian things became chic — but that didn't matter, the air was filled with the scent of flowering camellias (ages later, but only seven years really, we filled the back seat of a 39 Dodge with camellias — raided judiciously, no one's bushes completely stripped — on the night of our graduation from high school and enticed without any difficulty a whole line of girls in crinolines to leave the dance and lie on a bed of camellias) and the soft lap of water against the rotting wood of the dance pavilion.

I never believed that there could be a naval base so far from water, even after swimming across Mountain Lake (never found the mountain either), it might have been all of half-a-mile, and a reservoir at that; we had to swim hard, mainly so our feet wouldn't drag bottom, but that was useful too when we got up close to the base and frogmanned ourselves right up under the sentry's nose — and then back across, underwater as far as our lungs and bursting exhilaration at having penetrated the entire U.S. Navy, even if there were no ships, would allow and into one of our favorite creeks, hugging the limestone walls while sneaking along

25

the slippery bottom the object being to avoid stepping in the two-
inch deep water saying Guadalcanal was never like this. A few
years later, in Korea, I learned that in that, at least, we had been
right.

We needed money, of course. But that was easy. I got a dollar a
week working at Nolte's corner grocery after school on Thurs-
days and Fridays and from 9 to 9 on Saturdays—with deductions
for Cokes and candy bars; Mrs. Nolte kept score. Mr. Nolte had
a spastic right arm left over from a stroke he had had a few years
earlier and was unable to lift things like boxes and quarters of
beef; he was the butcher. Every Saturday morning he would drive
me to the packing house where we would walk among the hanging carcass halves until he found the right one—I never knew
why that one was righter than the others, something to do with
the proportion of fat; he would have it cut in two and I would fit
myself into the ribcage of the fore-quarter, carry it to the panel
truck, dump it in the back, wiggle out from under, and do the
same with the hind. I didn't mind the weight. I did mind having to sit on the seat beside Mr. Nolte jerking away at the controls—instead of watching the meat to see that it didn't slip
around too much there in back, I couldn't keep my eyes off what
was happening in front of the truck. Right then I always wanted
another job.

Still, all that spring and well into the summer—until I got a job
in a drug store, worked up to a dog kennel, finally hit the big time
as usher in a downtown theater three years later—my mother
got fifty cents for the house every Saturday night and I got my fifty
cents—minus deductions; that was plenty. Besides, there were
other ways.

You could take a streetcar to within a couple blocks of Kidd
Springs; fare for kids was three cents. There was, in addition, a
high point in the trolley line a mile from my house; if, at the stop
before, a stick was jammed into the cable reel so that the trolley-

arm would swing free at the high point also dislodging the stick and destroying the evidence, the driver would have to get out to reconnect the trolley; we could then slip into the open door and hide under a seat until time to get off.

And sometimes a sailor would give us a Coke. And sometimes — just now and then, not often — a girl in a cotton print dress would give us a Coke — and something indefinable would happen in an elusive location, perhaps between elbow and wrist where all strength seemed to fail or in the extensor muscle beside the thigh-bone where an increased gripping of the wooden rail could be felt, but the stomach refused the liquid Coke until the essential fluid had worked its way through head and chest and then it would take it in one slug absolutely rejecting it sip by sip. The only thing to do then was go into the water and off the high board out to the spinning tops and finally through the narrow channel under the footbridge connecting the pavilion to an island and into the lake with the ducks and geese. By then the last streetcar would have passed so we slept under a bush.

    Have you ever taught a girl to jack off?

    God no!!

Can they do it? I thought they had a hole. Maybe that monkey I saw jerking off in a cage at the roadhouse a couple weeks back was a female; it had a funny trumpet-like bell at the end of what I thought was its penis, maybe that's the hole. In the first wet-dream I remember, I was with a beautiful woman who had an organ like that monkey's. We stood, facing each other, penis inside something long with a floral bell at its end.

Ssao falls over backwards he is laughing so hard, but his arm, forefinger extended, continues to pump back and forth:

    tell her   tell her   she can't understand what we're
    saying   tell her

We are camped near Maun—Ssao, Damo, John, Kamko, Ku and Nai, and me—on our way to Tsodilo to do some work. My Norwegian friend, a NORAD volunteer at Maun Hospital, has joined us for dinner; several meters of boerwors[27] skewered on forked sticks have been roasting for an hour. We are—or were until just now—hunkered around the fire tending the meat, drinking wine, telling stories; at the moment we are all more-or-less in Ssao's condition, writhing in the sand helpless with laughter.

hey   you all   listen   you all   when i was still a young man not as old as Damo here or John   i went with the Mbanderu Tohoperi to sell some of his cattle at Maka-lamabedi   as cattle driver you know   the first time i had ever been past Sehitwa   we'd drive those cattle all day have to watch for lions at night   hot sun killed us always it is a long way you know   when we got to Makalama-bedi we could wash for the first time since leaving CaeCae i saw all those houses where you can drink kadi beer[28] and smoke dope   i had been to Qangwa   you know   they never buy many cattle there   at the time there were only few kadi houses at Qangwa   a lot of dope   sure a lot of dope   you could always get a lot of dope at Qangwa even long ago my father told me   i've driven cattle to Maka-lamabedi many times since   the last time a couple years ago   you know Twi i told you it was when you were away   police wanted to take me to jail for killing a porcu-pine without a license   i pretended to be a dumb Bushman who can't speak Setswana   they let me go   i even got the meat   but i was a young man that first time   i hadn't married yet   we stayed at Makalamabedi many days many days drinking   just going around seeing all those things   there i fucked a Goba[29] woman for the first time we were squatting around drinking kadi   just as now she said let's go   so we went into her house   there she lay down on her back   spread her legs with her cunt sticking out in front like that   i didn't know what to do

Ssao has leaned back, half sitting, his legs spread apart, patting his crotch so that we will be quite certain to envision what he describes.

> you know Zhu like to do it on their sides   you go in
> from behind with your belly against the woman's buttocks
> like this

His hand cupped slightly on its side, thumb against soft pad of forefinger, rocking on its wrist—back and forth. We all know this perfectly well—all except my Norwegian friend—but Ssao, a consummate raconteur, builds his story in graphic detail so that we are drawn thin in anticipation, adding comments when we can catch our breath:

> yes   hot sun kills you
> Really?
> no no   you lie

His arms shoot out in front of him; he slaps first one arm and the inside of its opposite thigh, then the other pair.

> she told me to lie between her legs like that   this one
> of my thighs against her's   the other like this   just in
> there like that   then she started bouncing up and down
> i didn't know what to do
> Yea!
> yao
> aie
> Aie!
> i just hung on   my eyes big   round   like this

The scent of camellias infused the lapping water of Kidd Springs while Makalamabedi opened its wonders to Ssao. The Springs covered no more than three or four acres: the lake, including the part on the near side of the footbridge which had a concrete bottom to form the official swimming pool, the pavilion, the surrounding park. The pool has been filled in, the pavilion replaced by a gym. A Japanese garden occupies a small part of the site. You are not supposed to walk on the grass. There are, of course, no more streetcars, not many buses.

Returning from Tsodilo, we stop in the bar of one of those places near Maun called safari camps:

> you should learn more Setswana so you'd know when somebody insulted you
>
> Yeah, I could tell they said something dirty. What was it?
>
> those guys   they live around here   they come to this bar maybe Whites will buy beer for them   one says he is a driver   they don't do anything   they asked why two old greyheads like us sit here letting those young men have the women   i said those are their wives   they said that doesn't matter   you can take them   you are a Bushman you know how to fuck sideways   that white man must know too   he speaks your language

People from other countries with something like a hundred dollars a day to throw around come to these safari camps to see what is left of the wildlife. They come in the dry months when animals are concentrated around a few bare waterholes. They want to see lots of animals.

Separate parts

The track is never the same no matter how often I drive it. The sun shines differently every day and the wind moves sand from east to west or west to east or from some other compass point that is predictable on a seasonal basis for the subcontinent as a whole but unknowable even from minute to minute down in the dunes and thornscrub. Aardvarks, pangolins, porcupines, mice, even ants and termites constantly change the contours of the tire tracks that constitute the road; the first two destroying the constructions of the last—all moving dirt, digging for food. In the dry heat centered around September-October some of that dirt, flour fine—called dust in English but more expressively in Zhu the separated part, the same word applied to divorce—turns to mud on the eyelids, each blink serving not to clean eyeballs but to renew the thin film which forms a fifth superfluous refracting surface (the other four being the powdered insides and outsides of windshield and eyeglasses) through which one learns to navigate much as a spearfisherman does not throw directly at an image under water, knowing not to look at a Namaqua dove flying parallel to the window and to glance quickly at a clutch of yearling ostrich easily staying ahead at 50 kph or a warthog tusker tiring after only a couple minutes at 40. A landscape of glances, monotonous, with compelling details.

I can cover the 320 kilometers between CaeCae and Maun in under seven hours when conditions are right; usually it takes longer. Once as long as four days—three of them stuck in mud, the rainy season state of the separated part accumulated in crotches of dunes . . .

January 76: returning alone to CaeCae; truck loaded with everything needed for the next five months—100 gallons of gas, cases of wine,

31

some food—mainly coffee plus beans and flour for bread to break the monotony of bush meals and sour milk—100 kilos of tobacco to be distributed along with laundry and bath soap, 200 tins of bully-beef and 75 bags of mealie meal for the Strasburg Supplementary Stuffing (to be fed in enormous breakfasts at my camp each morning for two weeks to a dozen volunteers, controls to insure that the results of glucose tolerance tests would not be skewed by undernourishment), the name in honor of generations of geese stuffed for their livers two tins of which are in my stock to be saved for lonesome Sundays. I had gotten through some treacherous places; more than once black muddy water had surged over the hood. The little puddle looked easy; didn't even gear down to first, two-wheel drive, riding on confidence: dead still, only a few hours left to the day, no use to try digging out now—time to celebrate the arrival of Sid's new tape[30] and Nancy's Christmas package which I had received in Maun her fruit cake along with a bottle of sherry dug out of the supplies. During the night, thunderstorms, half a foot of water added to the mud, in the morning only the tops of tires seen above the slush . . .

The way to extricate a vehicle from such a mess is to find a place near a wheel next to which a jack set on a plank carried against such a contingency can be forced under the axle, ratchet the submerged jack as high as it will go—the plank will be pressed into the mud farther than the truck is raised—stuff branches into the space created under the wheel, release the jack, watch everything sink into the mud (maybe two or three centimeters will have been gained), dig out the plank and fill its hole with sticks; repeat until you become convinced that more progress can be made at another wheel and begin on it; do not think of the fact that this one will have to be returned to. In practice, it doesn't matter which wheel is attempted first; each must be attended—again and again and again and again—working underwater, stripped to underwear. The idea is to build a column of logs beneath each wheel so that the truck sits above mud level and then to pave a path with branches through the remaining muck . . .

Hours of work showed me that alone it would take a week to get out so I walked the 28 km back to Kowrie, arriving with another storm and dusk. The three men who returned worked with me for two days jacking, digging, chopping until the unloaded truck, engine roaring at full power, shot out onto firm ground. Most of the case of sherry brought to hoard over five months was gone—gave the men the last two bottles for their road home, and there was a noticeable dent in the bully beef . . .

But the duration of the journey bears no relation to elapsed time, and like the wind is not predictable on the spot. Portents for today's drive were not promising: wine finished in the first four months fois gras down with the final bottles, five months is a long time on boiled meat mealie meal medila [31] a few lentils thrown in for variety, ready for Maun but reluctant to leave. Had three-and-a-half hours sleep last night, then drew blood from five to ten this morning—easy enough in itself, but a 6 km walk around the circuit of camps. My legs ache from squatting with right thigh horizontal to make a rest for the arms of subjects presenting their veins to be tapped. Then off immediately for Maun hoping to arrive before 6 P.M. in order to centrifuge the samples and take off the serum, the yellowish separated fraction containing cholesterol which Zhu recognize as the blood's fat. No time for coffee.

Everyone in good humor this morning, joking; saying I was stealing their chance to see who had the most fat this time. Too many samples today, hand cranking would take too long. As I was preparing to stick Tina, someone began to tell of the time in 1975 when she had said I couldn't get blood from her because her veins are so small and I had said yes, you are thin but you have a big vagina, realizing the slip as I spoke it—Zhu words for vein and vagina being similar—and turning uncertain whether or not to panic to her husband who looked at me deadpan and said Twi you know you shouldn't say things like that. I remember being very glad it is well known that I don't mess with women here; the decision not to enter into this aspect of community life made for policy reasons long before I arrived so as not to become enmeshed in factious jealousies. Not that the decision has been easy to carry out, more difficult as I became more thoroughly accepted here . . .

> the other day old Tsaa, a solid citizen we would call him, told me he wanted to speak a secret—if I liked his young niece, he would lend me to her. Lend me to her!

Luckily, I was well braced when reminded of that slip; Tina could have gotten the needle right through her elbow with my burst of memoried laughter.

> *The conjunctions that occur. They can't always be called coincidents; we select things, bias the course of future events. Still, they needn't surface simultaneously, juxtaposed in one certain way rather than others. Conjunctions: books packed for the field— it's true I picked up V because I know Pynchon weaves a kind of psychohistory of Herero into his writing, to read it in this atmosphere working and talking with Mbanderu. I didn't anticipate finding Jacob Marenga's name, John's father's father's older-brother killed in Von Trotha's Vernichtungs Befehl, 1904. The grandfather, the younger-brother, escaped with flesh wounds to settle later among the Zhu at CaeCae . . .*[32]

John, seventeen years old at the time, came to me one evening after first Carl then Lisa had gone home—I had been back in CaeCae only a few days, having delivered Lisa to the airport in Joburg—just out of the four day mud.

> you are going to be here alone every night now that your children are gone

> Yes, that's so.

> you'll be lonely   nobody to talk to

> Sometimes; I have books, a lot of writing to do.

> i'll stay with you every evening until you are ready to read or write or sleep then i'll go home

We joked about him that year 1975, not too kindly—Carl a year older, Lisa a year younger than he; I thought he suffered the retardation common to sons of preachers. We nicknamed him What, harsher but similar in intention to Knobe as he was called by everyone at CaeCae . . .

five years later when I would sometimes forget and call him by that name Ssao Damo or whoever might be present would correct me and say John isn't Knobe anymore—not after 12 hours a day times 270 days in 100° plus heat 10,000 feet down in the shaft 45 minutes in a packed cage called an elevator to get there another 45 to get back the remaining hours of those days in the brutal barracks of a Rand gold mine not after Nai for whom with that part of his pay that didn't go to his father he bought pretty cotton print dresses shoes perfume he and Damo had thought slacks worn by women in Francistown and Gaborone were attractive brought the first pairs to CaeCae for Nai and Ku John lived with Nai for more than a year took her with us to Maun and Tsodilo on our second trip wanted to marry her and her three children although it is nearly unheard of for a Mbanderu man to marry a Zhu woman ten years older than he until she abruptly harshly broke it off and he asked me many times why women did such things did they also do them in America hurting after Nai rejected him John would joke harshly pointing at Ku

see her   she likes to suck

How do you know? You've never fucked her.

she's my marrying cousin   i talk to her about it   if i want to fuck i go to my marrying cousins

Sure, I know. Damo, what do you think about this?

sure, after i'm dead

John chatting away beside me. I've only been half listening, thinking about my accumulated history here, John's talk unwittingly saturating my thought with our shared past, must be giving reasonable responses; he seems content—talk does keep my conscious attention on the track, wherever the rest may be. Beautiful driving today, going fast—we'll get to Maun on time—even with that banal song in my brain . . .

> *the feeling of running a perfect race moving with the gun arms legs lungs synchronized effortlessly smooth staying right on the curb no wasted body torsion . . .*

taking the deep holes, tires crossing just at the edges so instead of slamming into the far side they slide down into the holes pushing a cushion of sand beneath them, the Toyota rolling like a canoe cutting across swells in open water; the pleasure of driving with one hand steering, the other hand pressed against the driving arm's shoulder feeling muscles respond to the twist of the wheel . . .

give me your fingers   you've come   see my daughter

Yes, I've come; I'll stay nearly two years. She's beautiful, has your eyes. And another in your belly.

All through 75–76 we joked about the conditions under which we would sleep together; jokes made to defuse while expressing desire, always in the presence of others—her sister, mother, girl-cousins neutralizing the ground, diffusing the contact, making it less directly personal, giving room to be tender without compromise. The condition: stay here, be committed as we say . . .

When I returned six months ago she was married, to the same man with whom she stayed for a few months in 1975 before running away from her first try at marriage. Tina is finally getting the grandchildren she has wanted so long . . . this second child fathered by Ssao his affair with Glin his cousin well known and tolerated by his wife on the morning of its birth I went to Tina's camp to pay respects to the family although only kin normally see a newborn baby Glin asked me in the two lying inside a square tent enclosure of snow white sheets hung inside the hut outside Ssao asked whose nose the new one had and I called yours through the

walls this public acknowledgement recognized by Glin's Mbanderu husband who killed a goat that afternoon to feast the birth
of the child whose parent he remained . . .

It's more than policy now. I could buy in—make a proposal, in
current Kalahari terminology—my intrusion rationalized in discourse, to surface only occasionally in fights—say when hot dry
winds of September blow nerves raw and people quarrel anyway.

> Jesu! Did you see Tuga looking at me?
>
> she was drinking you
>
> Look, see me! I've been here a long time. Maybe it's OK?
>
> you could give her parents something   make a proposal
>
> what would Zhu say   they know you are going soon
>
> Uhn, you're right; forget it.

The shadow of colonialism hangs here still. What was it Sechele
said to one of the traders a hundred years ago?

> Look at your brother, white man; your preaching must
> be all nonsense; they take our native women up into the
> country as wives and are not married to them.[33]

It still goes on, often under a distasteful guise of liberalism, at
best a naive self-indulgence that goes home with stories of "my
enriching experience" while the remains of that experience are
left in a different context where memory and meaning are not the
same. In places like this everyone is enmeshed at least since ado-
lescence in negotiations for future commitments. Even among
themselves to break into, disrupt, these negotiations is called doing dirty, stealing. You don't read about romantic encounters between European and primitive facing each other over thousands
of years written by the victims. You read that things fall apart. It's
not a question of sex but of power—of disproportionate distance, of self-granted liberty to subvert context, to escape place
and process[34] . . .

I can't sing lost love songs colonially killed here where the discourse of dispossession is a daily force in life, where I am free to escape the dispossessed at will.

> The war between classes is
> A preliminary, provincial phase,
> Of the war between individuals.[35]

The colonial condition — in its neo form that is not new — continues to govern the encounter here; the struggle unequal, as it must be. And gender is almost an afterthought.

> *Doing dirty, creating reflexively a separation from self — burying knowledge under a burden of enlightenment, isolating the dirt insulating its reciprocal: a vaguely unclean feeling . . . the way I felt brushing-off Kora, who telephoned to say she wanted to keep in touch, because of a jealous woman sleeping in the next room . . .*

Damn!

Both front wheels into that deep hole where sand hides the first rocks: my mind shut down trying to wipe out that unwanted piece of the past eyes fogged over arms rigid foot frozen on the gas pedal, could have broken a spring. The guys in back will have bruises to show, tell me I didn't drive well today. Not perfect.

Words

My name-grandfather tells me things, often prefaced by

    this is something you should know
    those stars there those bunched together [the Pleiades]
    their name is Tchuum

    Does it mean anything, the name?

    no   it's something you should know

As is the fact that the Milky Way is the sky's backbone.

He is sometimes annoyed by the efforts of others.

    don't teach him that   it's half Mbanderu slang

An argument follows about Zhu grammar which I cannot yet understand completely. Grandfather prevails. He is serious about his language in a way very few speakers of any language are.

    this is something you should know
    mi ku ali a [I love-want you]

So,,,,, to love is to want; to want, to love. At first it seemed so simple, straightforward—at the same time a new idea; we—in what we, the same we, call the civilized world—like to think we separate the two concepts, different states of desire, calling them abstract nouns. Then it became clear: "I love ice cream" means simply "I want to eat ice cream as often as I can"—within limits dictated now by mirrors and thoughts of cholesterol; constraints imposed by modern means of self-awareness. For Zhu and Mbanderu—I'm sure for others living as they do—the truest expression of self-fulfillment is to be, if not fat, at least fully fleshed; loving and belonging expressed in sharing possessions and food. . .

Damo tomorrow when you and Twi go to Maun buy chisi
to bring to me   i love chisi   I want to eat chisi all the
time   this baby in my belly wants chisi   i love chisi [36]

And when we—the we in what we call the civilized word—
when we say "I love you" we imply possession, at least desired
possession. Grandparents make that clear, and Sunday School
leaves no room to doubt that if god loves us he wants us
exclusively.

To cherish: to love dearly, to hold in one's heart.

Zhu has an equivalent poetry: my heart wants you   my heart
weeps for you when it doesn't see you

And Zhu know that god's heart is dirty because he doesn't just
want us, he wants to eat us, therefore kills us; and does not weep
for us.

How to correct what I have just written? After writing it—
scribbling more insertions and deletions than first thoughts over
pages of my notebook, always a sign that thoughts are not composed, thinking: that isn't it, not the way to express what I want
to say—found Sartre's *Words* [37] among my books. He wrote of
his grandfather possessing the tiny world he begat around himself, molding his grandson; the reified air of the man's library.

> The reified air of CaeCae. There's no doubt I feel I be-
> long here: have lived as many days here as in any other
> place during my nomadic adult life—among so-called
> nomads who spend their lives inside a small circum-
> scribed space filled with kinship. Am I sincere? What
> does that mean? Could I be? How find the shifting fron-
> tier between possession and fantasy? Even here. Kinship
> —even here, where relatives are referred to as those
> who have each other—is often fiction, underwritten by

continually renewed reminders of obligation; both can be altered when expedient.

How convey these contradictions in writing? How dissolve the precious nobility that suffocates our image of these people? That deception that certifies our own noble descent. In a recent letter, Sven quoted someone—I've forgotten whom: everything you have learned is wrong.

Not a bad thing to remember here.

Perhaps that is it, after all. Perhaps a way to describe the commonplace of these things is to describe the banality of learning them—the trash that runs through one's mind maybe only through mine:

A chi ray	What may be
de mi ka say,	that I now see,
dum gay	there's a hole
in the Milky Way?	in the Milky Way?
what	where

Lying in the sand beside an unnecessary fire, sweltering in the night blackness below stars accentuated by new moon dark, mixing languages in doggerel. Damo understands—helping me learn Zhu he learns a lot of English; startled, he repeats

what   where's the hole

No, there's no hole. It's just that black space, there near the Clouds of Magellan, that looks like a hole.

Since there is no hole, the spirits of the dead—growing smaller through time until they disappear, reversing the process of life, replaced constantly by newly dead—will stay in the sky, harmless, their eyes the stars looking down on us, instead of coming down to bite their living relatives and carry them up where god will eat them because they weep for their absent kin and want their hearts to be joined again.

Different spirits must be treated differently. The eyes of newly killed gnus must be cut out along with the cheek skin surrounding the eyes so that they will be released to go up into the sky rather than stay behind as lookouts for their kin. Eland and cattle must receive a token of earth from the place where they died in the femoral socket on the right side of the pelvis so they will remember where to send their descendants.

That wasn't the only banality that Damo—and Tjitjo and John and Ssao—had to tolerate. Some they could appreciate: the sentimentality of a song like *Perfidia* translates into any language

> To you, my heart cries out, Perfidia,
> for I found you the love of my life,
> in somebody else's arms [38]

But one day, returning from the Namibian border: exuberant for forgotten reasons—carrying long, slender saplings cut as we went along to be used as roof-poles for Damo's new hut built in anticipation of the birth of his second child, the weight feeling good on my shoulder—when I burst into *Jersey bounce,* trying (ridiculously, it wasn't even funny) to make it sound like Ella, I had to say, no, I don't know how to tell you the words of that one.

Songs my mother taught me

The bones of the finger I used
to point out shadows to you—
shadows hidden in rock crevices,
next to knotholes on trees—

and to write my space on paper,
in the way that dogs and their kin mark a territory,
to tell you I have been here.

There is no need to follow.

But keep those bones.
Alone, they may show you things hidden
behind shadows I did not see.[39]

The time was different approaching the end of my sixteenth year
hitching the 200 spring-flowerfield miles down to College Station
to take the Opportunity Award exam that would let me go to
college two months later I won the half-mile city championship
for the second year running lost state by a shadow short enough
to put me on the Aggie freshman team in the fall of 1949. The
combined scholarships worth $400 for each of my undergraduate
years, enough to cover fees-room-meals in the mess hall (at the
training table during track season where we ate steaks instead of
"shit-on-a-shingle")[40] plus an allowance that almost covered the
cost of books. And there wasn't much to buy in that tiny central
Texas town or those around it, except beer dancing on cement
slabs behind roadside bars, and the Brazos bottoms were free for
dreaming—and hitch-hiking was free, except for those drivers
we had to pay by innovating lies about how much nooky we were
knocking; we tried to ride in pairs when the lift looked like it
would be like that.

Besides there were other ways.

You could collect Coke bottles left in the stadium after home football games at four-bits[41] a case (2¢ apiece for the 24 bottles and another for the pigeon-holed box); sometimes you could get $10.00 and that covered a real good date. But it wasn't plenty any more. So, in the summers I worked for a building contractor in Dallas; he was an alum who set aside jobs for Aggies who couldn't get by without work. I was aware enough even then to appreciate the implications of his paying us all union scale in open-shop Texas—CIO, "colored" men, college boys like me. Common laborer: ditch-digging, steel-framing, carpenter's helper, mortar man—I'd pick up two 98 lb sacks of cement one under each arm and carry them right up the ramp to the bricklayers' scaffold deck no matter how high

> *my first years on the beaches in the alleys under the houses raised on pilings above hurricane floods of Galveston prepared me well for such work—the cotton trade hit bottom during the Second Recession in 1938 when I was six my father unloaded banana boats I would often go with him trotting to keep up and play on the docks while he kept walking many times a day in a line of longshoremen up the gangplank then down again with a whole stalk on his shoulder for a dollar a day sometimes earning my keep too clearing away shrimp heads for the shuckers then carrying home a pailful of headless shrimp. That and the quarters of beef which must have weighed as much as a ten year old boy. Even the sedentary usher's job I got lying saying I was 16 when it was 1945 and I was really 13: at the time we lived in a place called Lisbon on the rural fringe about 8 miles from downtown Dallas when I worked the night shift it would be too late to catch the last streetcar home but I discovered that a freight which passed on the line 100 yards from our house left the city yard just after midnight so I would run the mile from the movie theater through deserted streets stopping at the beacon-like Dixie Creme lights making donuts for the morning hop the freight at*

the sharp bend where it turned out of the yard and the point of
the outside arc couldn't be seen from engine cab or caboose and
lie flat on my back on top of a car dreaming on the stars eating
every one of a dozen donuts before the train slowed at the crossing near my house and I could jump off. Later when I discovered
Chagal I realized that I had felt myself in the atmosphere he
painted.

> Songs my mother taught me in the days long
> vanished. . .[42]

She sang those words often and others from a vanished era.

Mami, how could Methuselah live 969 years;

she thought they must have reckoned years differently then but
how she didn't know—she did know that Chinese years are different from European and taught me to say "guni fat choy" and
count to a hundred and a lot of other things I've forgotten in
Cantonese, and that Passover occurred at different times each
year. Once I went to tell her that a colored woman was at the
door—the latest in a long line of Depressioned poor, white and
black, who came to every house no matter how itself poor asking
for work or a share of food—she told me that colored women
were ladies just like whites never mind that they were not called
that in the segregated South.

And she taught me not to hate anything British and gave me
English novels to read even though they had confiscated her
family's wealthy China-merchant life when the Great War broke
out in 1914 and put them all in detention camp in India where
her mother died after gallstone surgery and after the war was
herself sent to Germany where her twin-sister died of TB con-
tracted in the sanitarium where she nursed the sick and her languages got her a job as international telephone operator in Berlin. They were fed a lot of rabbits in the camp—so, she taught
me how to cook the small rabbits I shot and the large ones I
raised mostly to sell for Sunday dinners in those days when a
dressed chicken cost about as much as half a cow on the hoof—

*"two chickens in every pot" Hoover promised—but she would
never eat them, while my father put his trust in FDR and gave
me* One world *for my twelfth birthday.*[43]

> *Seldom from her eyelids were the teardrops
> banished. . .*

*I think those words of the song resonated with memories of her
own mother's final years—and they bore some relation to her
own years after my two year old brother died following surgery
to relieve hydrocephaly he never regained consciousness and was
sent home with a tube down his nose because we couldn't pay the
hospital and died one Sunday morning while I stood beside his
crib thinking his sudden spasms looked funny before dissolving
into tears of fear in the tension that followed—I was nine and
we had moved to Dallas just a few months earlier.*

It's great to be alive to work from 8 to 4:30—we parodied
the silly propaganda Bing Crosby sang to help keep the masses
whistling while they work but only out of earshot of those who
would do this all their lives.[44] Usually there would be no more
than two of us college boys on a job; those I liked were as aware
as I of our anomalous position—poor working class (my father
said we were white niggers) but awarded the opportunity to
belabor our brains and brawn into the middle or who knew how
much higher classes. . .

> Would you like to swing on a star,
> carry moonbeams home in a jar,
> and be better off than you are
>
> . . . .
>
> or would you rather be a mule?[45]

I would rather have the 1948 Pontiac convertible sitting on a
used car lot that I passed riding the bus home from work one day
. . . appropriately canary-yellow singing a siren song with jet-
black top red real leather seats; under the hood fan-blades filter-
housings head-studs and who remembers what-all else chrome-

plated—somebody had spent a lot of money on that car. So did
I—$800 for a start, my father co-signing my first bank loan; at
$1.07/hr it took a while to pay off. Somebody had also abused its
working parts so I spent a lot of time under it coaxing it to keep
going.

But I didn't care—kept spare clothes blankets pillows toothbrush
razor knives-forks-dishes in the trunk after work hit the Bar-B-Q
pit then out under the stars with buddies girls now in New Look
skirts too long in the post-war luxury of conspicuous waste
penny-loafers . . . top down letting rain fall in through warm
summer nights in the second year of our new war to again make
the world safe for democracy though we were told Korea was
only a police action.

> *Hurry on sundown and let's see what tomorrow may bring: the*
> *daily words of a white-haired "colored" laborer properly past*
> *the end of his toiling days necessity keeping him at it who spoke*
> *gently about life out of a lifetime harder than anything I could*
> *imagine—I hadn't yet realized that a black person born in*
> *Texas before Juneteenth 1865 [46] would have been a slave and*
> *the youngest would have been only 67 years old when I was born*
> *so that I must have met some of them, maybe on the Galveston*
> *docks—he wasn't old enough but his parents sure had been,*
> *history isn't that far behind us. I revered this old man as a*
> *philosopher and sat at his feet at lunchtime. . .*

hurry on sundown—
the Korean War and my senior year drew to an end together and
it seemed wise to accept another opportunity, this one offered
in the form of an ROTC commissioned 2d Lt rank complete with
orders to report for a year in Korea—which I could have dodged,
as ROTC itself had been a dodge, because Sus got pregnant in
the canary siren car or on its blankets and we had the twins and
Nancy on the way—to be (re)awarded by the GI Bill that let me
go to MIT, and

let's see what tomorrow may bring—

in the East where the sun now seemed to rise . . . in Cambridge I worked for Sert, TAC (for a brief moment directly with Gropius himself), Sasaki while I learned in one of my urban planning classes at MIT that social dimensions are inextricably intertwined;[47] fall 57, recuperating from several severe bouts of surgery, I took my advisor's advice and went back to A&M to complete my BA in one term rather than the two years it would take at MIT. I had only a seminar and a couple courses which left me free to browse in the library. One course was in Texas history which introduced me to Cabeza de Vaca and led me to Paul Radin's new *Trickster* (1956), and his *World of primitive man* (1955), Clark Wissler's old *American Indian* (1938), the Navaho stories of Oliver LaFarge (1963) and, more importantly, his work on Indian consciousness.[48] This led me eclectically to Reichart, Kluckhohn, and the work of the Cornell medical group at Cañon de Chelly. I had, until that moment, never heard of anthropology; I was most impressed to learn that by learning about others you could learn how to help them. I decided then—even before returning to the master's program at MIT—that my thesis would be a community development project on the Navaho reservation.[49]

Now I teach my children each melodious melody;
oft they flow from my memory's treasure. . .

having learned that no memory could be mine alone and if I tried to make it so I could not then recognize it for what it is, a texture of contexts common to and concurrent with others—transitive. My memories—of stories brought to me from China-Germany, of childhood, my education, what I learned failed to learn as a parent—inform my current observations because they resonate in my present, not because they occurred in some past called mine. A past that even I can reconstruct only in the bare outlines allowed by fragmented recollection—and then differently every day as old fragments rearrange themselves with new in different chords, and never recreate actual experience. So that memory is never wholly new but is always descended. . .

. . . vulnerable to any appropriation: as fallen fall leaves of trees —vivid colors sustaining perhaps each of us alone in the comfort of recalled contact. . ..

> When I see you
>   I'm told there are reasons
> why crocuses bloom through opened snow,
> and sometimes in fall out of season;
>
> distilling colors carried to the ground
> by autumn leaves,
>
> without a sound.[50]

But the past, always real in its own time, is now inert and of itself has nothing to offer. Discovering the past—more accurately, accidental parts of the past—is one way of enlightening the present; it is also one way of failing to be liberated from it—for example, by ennobling the present by reference to selected aspects of the past. And owning the past is a sure way of being enslaved by it—ownership requires partition, thus competition.

Selected, collectively compacted, the past supplies support for divisive ideologies . . . events and figures of history that might be made "cultural" for some but not others: language, or only the orthography of its written form; battles, particularly if selfhood can be claimed to have been trampled on the field of honor; heroes, the martyred metonyms inscribed with iconic signs; epic-legend-religion, the vehicles of sanctioned authenticity; material carriers of these mythic messages—dress, cuisine, utensils. We know of many collective celebrants of such selective, ethnopoeticized segments of shared history who solemnize that selection as their exclusive cultural property.[51]

Absurd.

Better to back off with Beckett:

> where I am, I don't know, I'll never know, in the silence
> you don't know . . .

better to speak gently out of a hard life;
better to teach how to cook rabbits and not eat them —

> . . . you must go on, I can't go on, I'll go on.[52]

From the age of 12, I wanted to be an architect. I did not intend to become an anthropologist; I wanted only to learn how to intertwine social dimensions in planning.[53]

Let us go then

On days with the right atmosphere—misty, or more likely, smoggy—in any case, diffused sunlight, blurred images, it looks like a giant Lorelei castle up on its rocky ridge containing too much of the world's gold. Valhalla in the sky. But, closer, inside, Joburg has harsh lines.

Harsher still is the journey there, made no easier by the fact it's necessary

                              —I
    need to kill and kill again
    my memory, turn my heart to stone, as
    well as practice skills gone rusty, such

    as to live, for instance. [54]

Departure forms at the border:

    rra, are you driving through to Joburg? can you give my
    sister a lift?

She stood there lovely, gentle, somewhat shy—later confided she too had evaluated, decided to take a chance; Botswana license plates are no more guarantee than others;

leers, surmise on the Republic side.

    can you stop at the next place?
    I'll try; maybe that one will be OK.

Painful to say to each other, who do not know each other,

    Maybe we both can't pee at the same station,

and

    ask a Black attendant for the keys.

A previous trip: two men, mechanics in a Gaborone garage, go-
ing to fetch a vehicle in Joburg gave me a lift. Among men there
is often greater reticence, or stoicism, in these situations; at the
petrol stop the sign WHITES is prominent but NIE BLANKES
is missing — and I cannot take what they are refused, and to
step later behind a bush would be capitulation. . .[55]

Go out a short distance from the city,
some sunny afternoon;
take a picnic or just go for a drive.

You will meet polished new school buses.
All you will learn about their passengers protected behind
    closed windows
is that they are white and seem as identical as their brown
leather satchels, though it must be admitted that some are now
    imitation.

But you will be able to distinguish the childern walking to the
    location
carrying books in plastic bags — the kind with shop names in
    large letters.
You will learn that a few are taught to beg with open hands,
and measure time by depth of expression rather than by size
    alone:
the larger, older kids will turn their faces from you or mutter
    something
you will not understand;
the younger ones, those with much still to learn, will smile
and wave in their joy of life.

And you?
I tell you, return the smiles
wave now
before it is your turn to extend your hands in supplication
when the bullets those childern learn to use in their real lessons
come looking for your blood — [56]

——I remember
Brazos bottom dust disfiguring black suits of colored men walk-
ing home in the heat of Texas Sundays; the women wore muted
rayons, passed along when outgrown. They walked on the left
shoulders of county roads and highways, keeping at least a body-
length from the pavement so as not to appear to be asking for a
ride. I always crowded the two-lane hitching to school. I remem-
ber lying on the grass in the city stadium the week before a ma-
jor track meet; sometimes the team from a Black school would be
there and our coaches arranged races; idly, we would ask our-
selves why we could not run against those boys when it counted
——one of our group said he got off on the thought of pregnant
nigger piss. I remember when I found out why: in the obscenity
of a sign hung from a dormitory window before a football game
against a university with one Black, in its law school. . .[57]

These memories are on my side of this road: kaffirs—wearing the blue coveralls symbolic of that name—walk, against the
traffic, keeping at least a body-length from the pavement. A
woman with a heavy headload and a baby in the blanket tied
around her body turns often for her two boys who race toward
the shiniest beer cans, their latest toys, thrown from cars owned
by Whites; Blacks drink cheaper beer sold in cartons. That's why
I cannot pick up the hitchhiker standing insistently on the narrow
pavement.[58]

I'm returning on Tuesday; here's my number. . .

She doesn't know Joburg but has been told where to catch the
Soweto bus, and calls that evening from a phone box in that place
where homes have no phones to say that she had found her way
and was well; unwilling to be swallowed by the slum to resurface
on Tuesday, unwilling to leave behind what is common on the
other side. . .

I search the faces I pass on the streets of Joburg[59]
though I can scarcely bear to look at them:

the pale facades behind which apartheid lies,
disguised by the routine monotony of business days—

interrupted now and then by laughter, even genuine joy,
and I wonder how that can be;

the dark facades behind which apartheid denies,
without expression, the routine monotony of servile
days—

interrupted now and then by laughter, even genuine joy,
and I wonder how that can be;

the shop facades behind which Africa dies
in endless variation—
as footstools made of elephant feet with zebra seats,
hooves of tiny antelope stuck on ends of keyrings,
and ostrich legs stiffened to support electric lamps,
to punctuate the rotting days.

And I wonder how it can be that these facades do not crumble
when they meet in the sun-scorched cauldron of Joburg streets.

And then I see the boy; not too surprisingly, at night there is always a boy huddled in the recess of the doorway I want to enter
to get a cup of coffee or something good to eat. . .

They say he is Black,[60]
but he is not so black as the stain
smeared in his tiny hand by the ton of coal
carried piece by stolen piece
to be sold for a cent in the dongas.

His hand would be beautiful were it not graceful from
hunger.

The hand seems arbitrarily connected to the head
thrust from a hole in grey herringbone rags
that once was a grown man's coat.

But his skin and bones feel deathly cold.

His eyes, dark as the stain on his hand,
grow large as the silver rand which suddenly shines
    there.

His small body, even in its poverty,
softens the harsh lines of Joburg.

The smell of strong, thick urine, the kind expelled by underwa-
tered kidneys, flows from the corner where he crouches in the
ragged coat several sizes too large (and now other thoughts
overlap those already slamming together: what happened to the
men who no longer fill those coats, and can't you see the awful
process of inheritance). The hand pleading from the rags, em-
phasizes the need within, as if emphasis were needed; sometimes the bundle tries to do nothing more than disappear into
the corner crevice.

Two responses only are possible after filling the hand; life does
not just go on, simply: turn away and walk the darkening streets
until conventional wisdom says they are not safe and then retreat
to my hollow room, or push in and order two, three times as
much as I originally wanted.

Freud and ethologists have had a lot to say about compensatory
eating. It helps neither me nor the boy.

We know each other now. Words come easier — some about how
to move through the barriers, some about what daily reality must
be for those who can't cross the border.

Some about the inescapable fact: there is no compensation for
those who go to their deaths clutching Passbooks to life, the bitter word Baas in their mouths, wondering where the next place
to piss may be.[61]

Given names

I felt I was on my way to hell
(but I didn't get very far)
           William Carlos Williams [62]

The journey can be just as harsh at home: atmosphere more likely smoggy from the window of the New York–DC Metroliner my mind's eye sees across the continent containing too much of the world's gold — looking like an endless paradise with spacious skies beautiful over amber waves of grain.[63] Yet, closer, inside, Columbia has harsh lines

> . . . the gem of the ocean,
> the home of the brave and the free,
> the shrine of each patriot's devotion,
> a world offers homage to thee.[64]

But,

> does the slightest trace of truth remain,
> running through the waves of grain . . .[65]
>
> Through other windows, commuter trains —

the names form a succession:

> Kingston
> Queens
> Princeton
>
> New Hope.

So much is obvious, required
rote material on any schoolboard map.

Barriers hammered to the water's edge,
hanging on to hope
in the way meanders prolong a river's rush.

Carlos understood.
Delivering his share, he looked for a mother
misplaced at the end of a waterway,
where the way
    is blocked
    and bridged.
    Broken,
the succession maintained.
A landscape encased
in the idea that everything can be controlled.

    Absorbed in what had been his father's place
            of private practice,
    a son dissects a legacy of papers
    and finds between the stratigraphic layers of
            a name
    a man he had not known in life.

In a resurrected station restaurant
a new Ladino, Carlos,
just arrived through Puerto Rico, perhaps
from another place,
thinks "eggs", wondering what he will get by saying that word.
While huevos fry behind his eyes
in green chilis and
            tomatoes (these, unknown to him,
            stripped of taste and texture in this
            Garden State
            to travel better in cellophane).

He eats what he gets.
Then descends the stairs into Trenton,
unaccustomed to the biting cold.

Clutching the name (kin to Carlos)
printed carefully on the paper in his pocket,
he fails to notice the cracked corn masa scattered around
    a twig,
which may yet grow amidst slowly shifting trash
that no amount of raking will retract.

           Sparrows peck up the corn;
           they see far in their adopted home.

All Saints, evening now,
red vigils on graves glow sharp as nails in the frost.
A gibbous moon—unopened door into heavens.
The dead, put where they are wanted, will stay.
The leaves of cemetery trees, all descended,
have been dumped into square steel containers
to be hauled to some alien place tomorrow:
    compacted,
    desiccated,
       someday the support of a new piece of pavement.

Carlos wrote closeted between patients

               . . . better to
              stumble at
               the edge
               to fall
                fall
              and be
            —divorced

from the insistence of place—[66]

And aligned himself with a river that rises no more than
forty miles from its fall, where Paterson was created en-
compassed in the bend of its arm.

Ladino, Carlos, backs away;
he hesitates
overwhelmed by the ordinary color of the poor.
He shuts his eyes.

Time is running out for him.
The sparrows are flying toward silhouettes of trees
blown black against a receding sky.

      Carlos will drown,
      as he drowned before,
      as he will continue to drown without knowing why

where the Passaic is lost in the mouth of the sea.*

---

*A note on geography is called for here: the Passaic River empties into Newark Bay
the waters of which are diffused around Staten Island, on the north side through the
Kill van Kull into the Upper Bay of the Hudson in which the Statue of Liberty stands
on its island. The allusion is to the unequal light that beacon shines on the paths of
immigrants: for those, like me, who are—however poor—certified white Europeans, the light shines bright with opportunity, even during economic depressions;
for others, especially those of warmer color, it glows correspondingly dimmer.
William Carlos Williams, who had an ambiguous relationship with his Puerto Rican
mother while exalting American democracy in super-Whitmanesque terms, seems
an apt metaphor for these disparities—a metaphor that takes on added cogency in
the current political atmosphere in which immigrants to America must struggle for
rights and opportunities.

Killer chill

it was called in the headline set in 74-point newspaper gothic:

JOHANNESBURG, TUESDAY, JULY 1, 1980 *(Rand Daily Mail)* Eleven people are reported to have died of exposure in Johannesburg since the start of the weekend victims are black their bodies were found in Mondeor Bez Valley and Alexandra Township during the past three days police say some of the dead were found frozen to death in the open on Sunday morning in a chill development in the wake of the deaths yesterday coal merchants reported a shortage of anthracite supplies that has been described as the worst ever Alexandra has been hit hard by the shortage and at the Wynberg coalyard on Friday supplies ran out

while

GOLD soared to $662.50 in London yesterday morning the highest level since February 21 the Chamber of Mines announced yesterday that new rates will raise the minimum starting pay of black underground workers on all gold and some platinum mines to R100 per month minimum starting pay for surface workers will rise to R75 a month all black miners receive "free board and lodging" said the statement "similar" starting rates and increases would apply in the coal mining industry some "liberals" are believed to be disappointed arguing that a greater effort could have been made to raise black wages in the light of the dramatic rise in the gold price

John told me of needing money while I was away in 1977–78 he signed on a nine-month contract and one day watched men die under a roof-fall at the mine-face of a deep gallery in

Dornfontein he carried water for the white gang baas which he wasn't allowed to drink for R90 per month several thousand meters underground before this year's raise or else he might have been under that roof while Damo joined the South African army needing money

also on the same front page of the *Rand Daily Mail* for Tuesday July 1, 1980 the ban imposed on the eve of 16 June (four years after Soweto)[67] against gatherings of persons

at which any protest or boycott or strike is encouraged or discussed or which is held in protest against or in support of or in commemoration of anything

was extended for two additional months and applied to 45 rather than only the original 24 magisterial districts including Johannesburg (in which are Mondeor, Bez Valley, Alexandra) and Wynberg

Special to the *New York Times* WASHINGTON, March 28 [1981] President Reagan was "showing the way toward a better tomorrow for all Americans government's first duty is to protect the people not run their lives . . . (contd)

while

Village Voice March 25–31, 1981: in Brooklyn Sally Brazell 59 year old hospital worker was found dead in her heatless home on January 20 and is believed to have died two days earlier she froze to death the landlord Joseph Kotler failed to provide heat for the 54 black hispanic and elderly jewish tenants in the building—

I don't think people are entitled to any services, says Budget Director Stockman in the same *NYT*

—in a civilized city landlords like Kotler would be prosecuted for negligent homicide instead the tenants have to sue him.

That's good but it's quite a different thing for people to demand that they have a right to a certain amount of income or services, Martin Anderson, the president's chief domestic advisor quoted again in the same *NYT* . . .

(contd) . . . they don't seem to care that if we don't move in the bold innovative way outlined by President Reagan this country will face an economic calamity of unprecedented magnitude the Vice President maintained while showing the way to tomorrow;

and elsewhere the Administration says that services chopped out of the Federal budget can be supplied by the states or business,

or volunteers.

There is no place to stay warm inside.

Two men both apparently homeless froze to death on city streets on Christmas morning as the temperature here fell to its lowest level in almost two years (*Washington Post* December 26, 1980)

But I ain't crying in your Boston cold, mon. I'm just waiting for my turn to come and it don't be mattering where. 'Cause the problems of South Africa are the problems of Haiti and the problems of Haiti are the problems of Roxbury: politically exiled Haitian lawyer (*Real Paper* March 19 1981)

The sun no longer shines for me with its same beauty;
songs of birds do not sound their same sweetness.
The sight of the city across the water from its Harbor
    Islands is overlain in my eyes
by cracked mosaics of decaying pavement:

and I don't know if I should be embarrassed or ashamed
to breathe air that others may breathe
to hear songs that others may hear
to see a sun that others may see
                    in a land where
                    I walk in a warmth that they are denied
                    I talk in a light that to them is a lie,

where I smell the silence of the cold dead
breaking apart.

A card with landscapes

Returned to camp towards noon, a morning of walking begun before sunrise: inspecting snarelines of one of the few men who still hunts here, counting animal spoor along a transect established in 1973. Dealing with death, and the arrangement of it, as an unremarkable routine in everyday life. Snares set for steenbok and duiker, for ostrich, and for birds of the pheasant family. Bucks eluded the snares; ostrich had not been attracted. Only one bird caught, a korhaan. The bird, too tall for the spring-stick, was not lifted off the ground; struggling, it had torn its skin loose at the gullet. The skin rolled up the length of the long, thin neck. Before dying, the bird had wrapped itself around a fallen dead branch.

The four women whom I employ to monitor menstrual cycles were waiting to make their daily reports. Also waiting, a small bundle of mail, the first in six weeks. A truck had arrived in the night, bringing diesel fuel for the well-pump; it had also brought the mail. The bundle put aside in deference to matters of higher priority: reports of the monitors; transferring the morning's data to permanent record books so that the meanings of shorthand jottings made while walking, looking, measuring would not be lost; a man arrived, arm at his side, index finger extended as if pointing accusingly at the earth—pouring blood transformed the finger into a foot-long tapered red candle dripping in the heat, a section of bone exposed in the fleshy pad—I had to put it back together; a request for advance payment for next month's spoor count on a distant transect—the money needed to drink beer and whisky delivered in the same service truck—it would have been hypocritical to refuse.

A postcard and a letter bearing the same return address were in the bundle of mail. Reading the letter, I may have murmured: Which Jane? Perhaps it was only an expression on my face. Ssao, who had come into the hut to get sugar for the tea he was brewing, asked: what's wrong. I told him.

> Dear Ed,
> I have been saving this card for a month, hoping for a post 4 June address
>
> . . . .
>
> Eating pastries every day; running to take them off. A huge indoor picnic today; raining. I love being back in Ann Arbor, but hide out to work.
>
> More later,

A color reproduction of Emil Nolde's *Frisian Landscape.* Jane knew how attracted I am to the marshes of upper Michigan, knew too that this attraction grows from an ancestral attachment to the somber Baltic coastline, stories from childhood; knew that I am irrevocably drawn to those places where planes of boreal ocean, land, and sky intersect—the blues, greens, greys of weathers there—that for me, gorgeous desert sunsets are no substitute for pale northern twilight.

Dated 30 June. Received 31 July.

Jane had been dead eleven days.

Killed by a speeding drunk careening out of control from Ypsilanti: Bomber City, where the Second had been manufactured for Böll on the Rhein.[68] When I read that she had been buried next to Leslie White, I could no longer avoid knowing which Jane.

Ssao told Damo and John. They brought their tea, coffee for me. Asked what sort of person Jane had been, how she had looked, I told them about her work on Cyprus, that it was similar to mine here, that we often spoke of our respective places, that I had told her about them. Did she have children: no. A husband:

yes, it was his letter that told me of Jane's death. Had we been lovers: no. . .

> *two years ago, crossed legs on the floor of my apartment one midnight, knees touching over some morsel Jane had brought, taking a break from work; talking of sexual fidelity, how it is merely part of the larger fidelity to oneself, that in this as in other important things ad hoc decisions betray an unfinished integrity. . .*

let's go to the Mbanderu camp to drink

Only four beers remained, one for each of us—but a whole bottle of whisky, killed buying capfuls for each other. Drinking in a very large hut still under construction: all browns—ochers of skinned roof-poles and thatch; damp umber of drying cowshit on the walls; ash tan of sand where the floor had not been laid; chocolate-black Mbanderu; bronze Zhu; even the white man burnt siena. A stash of grass had been included in the cargo.

Why did the sun shine through the unfinished thatch onto the only blue cap in the place?

We slept the afternoon into evening—I in the open bed of the Toyota into which I crawled in a futile attempt to escape the flies and the vision of Jane's lifeless body hurtling through the air. Reliving the scene I did not see: the re-creation made imperative by distance and the delay in knowing. Without some kind of experience of it, the scene could not be real.

> The letter bearing reality said: it would be better if we were together.

Two days before I had made cheese—not unlike the soft white cheeses of the Mediterranean; sliced that night with garlic in olive oil, bread baked in an iron cooking pot, red wine

> in memory of Jane Sallade.[69]

And these shall be the signs

They shall cast out devils . . .
they shall lay hands on the sick
Mark 16:17–18

Nisa, age seven months, died during Passover 1976; the day was
Good Friday by a rival reckoning. Such fine distinctions in relat-
ing the position of a full moon to the vernal equinox are understood so well here, where divisions among kin are symbolically
mediated. . .

I should learn how Muslims inject meaning into this part of their
calendar — to clarify, for me, those modes of distinction. . .

Strange. Sounds of singing from the direction of the molapo; there's
no camp there. It's adults, not kids; starting in mid-morning. Odd.

Twi   come   bring medicine

Where?   Who's sick?

there   by the molapo   Nisama has big sickness

aie aie
it's bad
i'm hot   i'm boiling
i'll die
my wife help me   Kushe gets up and sprays water
                                    from her mouth onto Ssao who
i'm flying   i'm too far   is entering trance to fight god
i'll die   for Nisa's life
it's bad
my wife's mother my
mother's cousin

help me   Suona gets up rubs the flat
palms of her hands on
Ssao's body

Shit I forgot sugar she won't take the bitter aspirin and penicillin.

Kamma, Tishema, run bring sugar; you know the box I keep
it in, with tea and coffee—maybe there's a little honey; bring
that, it's better.

It's a virus I'm sure the antibiotic won't do any good maybe protect her against secondary infection anyway the aspirin will bring
her fever down.

Ssao's tensed forearms shro me as I work Kushe Suona Kuna continue to clap with their hands the beat and rhythm while singing the
song without words I don't dance this time knowing they want the
medicine I bring not what I learn from them Nisa swallows the sweet
syrup eagerly encouraged by fevered thirst Ssao rubs his sweat on
us all.[70]

aie
it's bad

your old male cousin   Ssao addresses the child without
naming it or using a kin term;
Nisa is a classificatory child of
his because her mother Dikau is
in the relation of possible wife
to him

that one whose father's father married your grandmother's father's mother   that one Tika   he is the one
he with your other cousin   that one whose father is
your aunt's husband's older brother   that one also
married to Tika's older daughter   that one Kamko
those two killed the python the big female python sleeping in the waterhole   the one that guards god's waters
those two killed the python and ate it

Dikau sits apparently passive (but I take her pulse: 140—hating this role of always investigating—cradling Nisa in her lap while Kushe Suona Kuna minister to her an ointment of oil extracted from sour plum seed-kernals mixed with charcoal from the burned seed-shells forefingers applying the form of a cross to the child's forehead and chest. . .

Is it possible to know if that cross originated in Palestine rivalries 2000 years ago brought in the nineteenth century by Rhenish missionaries to this corner of the Kalahari. . .

she continues to sip my sugared aspirin all of our arms simultaneously tangled around the tiny body Ssao's the women's and mine.

>   it's bad
>   my strength is gone   Ssao collapses and lies motionless
>   in the sand.

Nouo va eta ku je omundu omboro . . . ama tja ku je Efata okutja Faturuka

Marenga had read two-three Sundays ago

> And they brought to him a man who was deaf and had
> an impediment in his speech; and they besought him
> to lay his hand upon him. And taking him aside from
> the multitude privately, he put his fingers into his ears,
> and he spat and touched his tongue; and looking up to
> heaven, he sighed, and said to him, Eph'phatha, that is,
> Be opened.

>   it's sort of strange that he uses spit   i don't know
>   about that   but in pictures he is always wrapped in
>   clothes like a Mbanderu woman   maybe he can't
>   easily get to his sweat under all those clothes

Ssao tells me

>   old people saw that white people had real power be-
>   cause like Zhu they know god   Jesu and Kqo are
>   the same   Satana and Ganwa are the same   Jesu
>   wrestles with Satana for peoples lives just as we

69

> medicine-keepers wrestle with Ganwa   when a
> person dies the spirit comes out in the breath   you
> know the huvf sound the last breath makes at the
> time of death like when we kill a goat   that spirit
> starts up the sky path   the road to Ganwa's place
> is wide

he draws a swath with three fingers in the sand

> that road is easy   the road to Kqo's place is hard

he draws with one finger in the sand

> Satana stands at the crossing eating flies   trying to
> catch dead people   not many escape[71]

Nisa died two days later. A respiratory virus was prevalent in southern Africa at the time; two other Zhu infants—one at Tshumkwe in Namibia, one at Dobe—died in that same week. The python was killed at Ggo, a pan the ownership of which has been in dispute for at least two generations. Tika and his family undoubtedly have longer-standing rights there; they are not people of CaeCae but of the East. Yet Nisa's family has been acquiring cattle for some time and enlarging its active range of land use. Kamko, married to Tika's daughter, had divided loyalties. Now, because the child's death was attributed to a transgression by her in-laws, her family gained advantage in its claims to Ggo. Shortly thereafter, Tika's daughter divorced Kamko and became the mistress of a Tswana man whose family claimed legal ownership of Ggo—Tika's family had been their servants for generations.

John asked if I had spare mealie meal to contribute to the wake; I didn't but gave my last, nearly full, 12.5 kg bag knowing I would find a way to replace it or substitute—calling on my circle of reciprocity—during the remaining weeks before going to Maun again. Kanah, Kamko's second cousin, who owned the largest flock of goats in that network, was obligated

to supply a big ram (this one's useful life nearly finished anyway Kanah surely thinking already of advantageous ways to
get rid of it). The boiled fat—poured over mealie porridge
—restored strength to us all. No one from Tika's family was
present.

Rain

Seemingly endless days of dripping rain are both welcome and dreary here, just as everywhere. In some years—perhaps two out of five or six, sometimes none at all for five or six years in a row, sometimes two or three back-to-back—February can be like that; by mid-March people are weary of the constant damp. Termites claim the poles and thatch of huts built on too-shallow dunes, where compacted sands of melapo are strong enough to support underground tunnel structures; a gritty residue sifts down—wood dust from their chewing, sand from tubular passageways cemented with termite spit constructed to shield their makers from the sun as they work their ways up walls to the roof. Such a hut needs to be beaten: its contents taken out and its roof and walls flayed—as we used to beat carpets hung over backyard clotheslines with brooms. Boxes, anything gnawable, must be balanced on rocks, old oil filters saved for such use when replaced, gotten off the ground. It's best to abandon such a hut and build a new one.

Clothes and bedding stay wet, reinforced by sweat that can't evaporate in the muggy heat; mildew invades leather; sinew bowstrings become soft and slack; arrow and spear bindings unravel; seldom-used wooden utensils grow green mould and must be discarded. Drowned flies float in cups of coffee.

Here there is no Groundhog's Day on which to say maybe in six weeks the sun will break through and daffodils bloom. But other things are said that mean the same:

now shortly   in a month perhaps   when moon returns
to this phase to this position up there   now shortly it
will be Tobe when nuts and fruits will be ripe and garden

melons   sun will go along its north path   will not be so
hot   there will be days days days days days without rain
we will take horses to hunt eland and giraffe   it will be
fat times   we will pick a few green mealie [72] ears just to
taste them   will leave most standing on the stalks until
the cold of Guum begins when you can chew on the boiled
hard kernels of a single mealie-cob from mid-morning till
noon [73]

Before the end of April, the wet season begins to blow away; you
can watch it go. Clouds form in the afternoon heat at the tops of
thermal columns — evaporated from the moisture in the sand —
to be carried westward by upper winds, removing water from
the land. As the sun sinks, its heat is deflected, evaporation stops,
and at twilight the sky is clear again; by mid-May, when Guum
begins, there is no dew. . .

In 73, rains began early—at the end of the second week of October
—after three years of severe heat and drought. I had thought the
vegetation could never recover and didn't believe Manuel's descrip-
tion of CaeCae in the rain. The wells went dry on seven days that
September. Returning from his snares, on the day I caught the tortoise, Zona took a different direction—straight to a rainpool called
Kkao zzi, hyaena shit; while we walked, he shoved a stick into the
body of the tortoise—between carapace and plastron, the upper and
lower shells, where the tail and hind legs come out—and now he
stuck the other end of the stick into the sand beside the pool (the
animal's legs continuing to walk uselessly in the air—hours later it
was still alive when put to roast in ashes); without a word, Zona
stripped naked and walked into the knee-deep, opaque water—I was
just seconds behind—and silently, with only an occasional grunt of
satisfaction, or a murmured this is good, we scrubbed our skins and
hair with handfuls of sand scooped from the muddy bottom. . .

Life is more relaxed at the cattleposts set up beside the larger
rainpools than it is at comparatively crowded CaeCae when all
the people and cattle of the place are here during the five to ten

months when there is no water in the pans—some years there is never water in the pans but occasionally, rarely now, it is possible to stay out for most of a year; people say that in the past such years occurred more frequently. Each cattlepost belongs to specific families, Mbanderu and Zhu, who look upon themselves as belonging to each other—fictively extended families, sometimes with a few real common ancestors. Everyone lives in old-style grass huts—small ones, some so small their entrances must be crawled through—used only for storing the few items brought out to the posts and for sheltering from heavy rain; ordinarily, everyone sleeps outside.

The atmosphere must be something like the better folkloric elements of the Old West. People dress more casually, are not so concerned about modesty; women tease their men about exaggerated contortions while in trance; men play a highly animated version of scissor-paper-stone, saying of the loser that he has become a woman. There is constant movement between cattleposts and CaeCae; everyone riding donkeys—mothers and fathers with a child or two in front on the donkey's shoulders, between the reins; sometimes another, older, child behind the saddle.

I don't ride donkeys. Donkeys and I don't understand each other. I ride horses. . .

Returning from the rainpool at Ggo in March 76, grandfather's big bay stallion, that catches giraffe and eland easily, wanted to run; told Tjitjo, Damo, and Ninnow that I would gallop ahead get a fire going in the hut because a heavy rain was blowing in; they would follow on their slower donkeys. More than six miles to go, but that horse, well over 17 hands, never slowed. . .

two weeks later he was lamed going after a small female eland stepped in a springhare hole throwing grandfather spear run through the length of the man's right calf by the time I saw it the wound needed reaming with a stick wrapped in cloth soaked in iodine the horse's lame leg bathed with gasoline within a month both were hunting again. . .

Had the saddle and bridle off in a single motion as I dismounted, sour-milk biscuits baking in the iron pot when the others arrived soaked and shivering. Drinking coffee with brandy, eating biscuits with honey —the honey from Maitso along with five birds given in anticipatory exchange for dresscloth he asked me to buy for his wife Tasa—Tjitjo asks

> how can i find out what a white woman is like
>
> Get a white woman. But be careful; some have very long pubic hair, and a lot of it. You might not like that.
>
> what's this   long hair on the cunt   i can't even grow long hair on my head   you lie   it's not possible   how could you get through it
>
> Doesn't make much difference. I like the salty ones. . .

that cement slab song in my head

> Let me be your salty dog
> or I won't be your man at all;
> honey, let me be your salty dog.[74]
>
> don't know about salty ones but i know a lot about honeyed ones (Ninnow, 53 years old) . . .

Some of my friends have had opportunities to make comparisons —with the Old West; when in Maun, we often go to films shown at one of the safari camps, many are westerns. Kamko's first was *Butch Cassidy and the Sundance Kid;* Damo, Ssao, and John were there. Translating, I kept up a continuous jabber

> That man, he loves the girl and . . . now those two are trying to get away from those guys who are following their spoor. . .
>
> shutup   we can see what's going on

see Kamko he's looking closely   seeing things   tomorrow he'll paint about this

He did; painted the most lyrical moment of the film: the bicycle
scene, handstand, backwards on the handlebars; but Kamko, unlike Damo, understands not a single word of English.

About this same time, he painted a rainbow ending in a pool of
water—the one I ran to photograph against a sunset reddened
sky almost as saturated with color as the rainbow itself, not knowing Kamko was painting it in his camp a kilometer away; later, we
talked about seeing the same thing from different places. We often talked about seeing; that to look is not enough, you've got to
put yourself in the looking. Once, Ssao asked why he had painted
no trees, no landscape, no base of ground or grass with a pair of
giraffe

that's what i saw   if you try to put something in that you
don't see it will be wrong [75]

Snakes are the protectors of rain; the penalty for disrespect can
be severe: Nisa's death was divined to have been retribution for
the killing and eating of the python at Ggo. In the hot, rainy
months snakes give live birth and are seen often . . . Chwama,
young 13 year old Chwa, brought part of a decaying duiker, killed
by a mamba bite, from a day's gathering—Old Man Gau said to
me, see that   Kumsa tells he has seen that a female mamba has
her young on Woman Rock—the warning implicit but clear:
avoid that place for now. . .

Throughout southern Africa, they have been associated with
rain, pythons and mambas; it seems may have been so far into the
past: snakes with horned heads and human limbs are painted on
cave walls at Giant's Castle high on the Drakensberg (Dragon
Mountain—did Europeans transfer mythology to the southern
end of Africa); horned snakes are painted too on the bare rocks

of the high Brandberg (Burning Mountain—flame-red in the setting Atlantic sun, 90 km to the west, from whose flanks can be seen at night the light at Cape Cross claimed by Portugal in 1484). Some of these paintings are a thousand years old and more (on Mont Parnassus Apollo slew the Python risen from the deluge, horned serpents adorn Egyptian temples; is there a substrate of myth shared across the continent), and all are far away from where Kamko had yet been; but, one day—before either he or I had seen old paintings on rocks—he painted snake-persons for me.[76]

At Tsodilo, where, too, horned snakes are painted, a deep hole extends far back into the rock holding a permanent pool of rain water: Samanchai said the big mamba that lived there guarded the pool against those to whom god refused the water, but the snake wouldn't hurt anyone who respected it. He had once found a leopard dead in the pool, killed by the mamba. Ssao John Kamko Damo agreed such things were true; while a ten-foot mamba, thick as my arm, slid slowly toward us, no more than two meters away, and curled under a rock.

Only much later—telling about it in a city, the foreign atmosphere adding an absent danger—did I think of the fear that was supposed to be there.

A conversation with Kahai

Kahai arrived from Namibia a few days ago, came to greet me this evening:

> tonight i'm going to tell you many things i'm happy you are here again as i was traveling the road home i heard you had come when you did not return for such a long time i thought you must be seriously ill then i became afraid god had taken you every time the sun set blood-red we said maybe you were the one who was dead now i know you had very bad malaria-fever so i'm happy you could come back i think you must have two places one in America and one here just as i have this place and the one where my father was born in Namibia every person has two places stay there for a time and stay here for a time you have a fine house and camp here you should have someone look after it when you go live in it to keep it well so it will be ready when you return every time another thing you should not kill all your cattle at Christmas buy some young cows with horns like this as long as your hand in addition to big oxen the cows will give you calves in addition to milk so you will not have to spend money to live here do you remember Masharo[77]

I remember what you told me before, and I have read Norna's books. I know his son, John; we live in the same place in America.

that's good i'm happy do you see him there

Yes.

when Masharo and Jonni came to Onyainyai i was living there Harara and i were there you know our wives are cousins

we became good friends exchanged many gifts as good friends
should   later because water diminished we took our cattle
to Kaura   Angelica-father[78] went there but i stayed   then
the Burusi[79] were trying to drive us back to Botswana   they
shot many of our cattle   they shot 108 of my cattle   Jonni
took many pictures of the dead animals[80]   that's when i
returned here to stay at CaeCae   at that time i had a young
boy living with me his name was Samqo   young-Samqo   he
was about so tall   if you stood up his hair would be where
your ribs begin   i had had him with me since before he was
weaned   his father and i worked together for many years
you remember that my Zhu name is Samqo   i am that Samqo's
name-grandfather   i gave him his name   i lent that Samqo
to Masharo to help him   when i had to come back here because the Burusi would not let us keep our cattle in Namibia
so we had no way to live there in the place where our fathers
were born Samqo followed me but i told him to go stay with
Masharo   now he has a good job at Tshumkwe   i want to
lend Gao to you so you can take him to America to go to
school   he has good brains and is not too old to learn

The term "lend" has different connotations in Zhu and Mbanderu
than it has in English. The daughter of the richest man at CaeCae
—a wealthy woman in her own right, yet forbidden by her father to marry and thus remove her cattle from the homestead—
has as her name of reference Makademai (Borrow Me): from a
proverb about the spirit of a child calling down from among the
ancestors in the sky to prospective parents in her lineage on
earth, borrow me for a time so that i may be among you before
returning here.

Walk with a Mbanderu man as he drives his cattle to pasture
or ride with him hundreds of kilometers from where he stays, if
the burial place of a male ancestor is passed—even long after the
ox-horns have been eaten by worms and ants and the gravestones

removed by other people   the site is remembered, marked by a
living tree—the dead person is addressed by a kin-term:

> ii   moro   moro   moro   bashandanke. . .
> yes   greeting   greeting   greeting   i thank you deeply for
> the cattle you have sent to lend me   as you have seen
> they are well cared for   they will continue to be looked
> after vigilantly but you must send more   protect me on
> this road to that other descendant of yours to the place
> where i am traveling   let me find much milk there and
> much meat   yes

i want to lend Gao to you—you can take him to America to
go to school

But you know there are problems. Gao may become lonely
and want to see his people.

yes it's certain   he will   just as we cry to see your children
Bau and Ninnow who were here   one wants to see one's
people   but you must take some of us to see him from time
to time   his father also Tjitjo and his wife should go   and
you can bring him to see us each time you return

But, there are problems, too. You have told me of the things
you heard in Namibia; those things may become worse instead
of better. We are right on the border. Someday the government may not allow me to return.

gorumenti can't stop you   when two people meet both may
lie dead on the ground   only one may fall   or they may continue to walk together in the same place   it doesn't matter
it will be god's will

The gospel according to Mark

Go ye into all the world, and preach the gospel to every creature
Mark 16:15

In 1842, the Rhenish Missionary Society applied this evangelical command to the land of Zhu and Mbanderu. The German word tuch—cloth, kerchief—entered Mbanderu (also Zhu) as duku along with grey, neck-high, long-sleeved, sand-length Rheinland fashions that replaced the modesty of bare Mbanderu woman-skin. Missionaries were point men in the corruption of the country, believing in blasphemy; twenty years later every headman had his Euroam trading partner who provided too few guns (just enough to keep them on the string) and a little ammo (just enough to keep them fighting the Nama, who also had their company traders, diverting their attention from orderly conquest of colony) along with cloth tinpots glassbeads. Boer ranchers trekked in right behind.

yes i have a wife   she's visiting her family   yes i have a son he's this tall (indicating the height of a boy about 10 years old)   he's with his mother   she'll bring him soon

> twibo mima kaise khona mi ye twibo
> twibo mima kaise kala mi ye twibo
> twibo mima kaise tobe mi taa twibo
> twibo mima kaise kala mi gxum twibo
> twibo mima ka shii mi ye twibo
> twibo mima shii khona mi ye twibo
>
> my twibo first ruin me ye twibo
> my twibo first screw me ye twibo
> my twibo first borrow my prick twibo

> my twibo first screw my cunt twibo
> my twibo now fuck me ye twibo
> my twibo fuck ruin me ye twibo

Young men—my guys visiting Dobe with me are the catalyst for local bloods to show off their special attraction—taunt him and laugh the sidemouthed laugh of derision; they sit and offer him kadi-beer they know he won't drink (they've seen him plenty of times before) and when they can control their convulsions they shout

> hey you got a wife hey
> hey you fuck her hey   hey
> hey you got a child

Old people fill tobacco pipes in silence moving aside in an effort not to notice young women some with babies on their backs dance and pantomime in circles around him hilarious kids dance too persuading him to join in his own ridicule singing himself

> twibo mima kaise khona mi ye twibo

His name is Twi, same as mine, they call him Twibo; he wears men's clothes but associates with women, does women's work. He has no wife, no child, has never slept with a woman as a man. . .

> when he was so big [indicating the height of a boy about 10 years old] maybe 30 years ago Timo tells me between snickers a bunch of Boers around the farm where he lived in South West took him to the bush and raped him in the asshole   they did this many times   maybe for two or three years   nobody knows   he stopped telling   his mind had gone

Twibo looks at no one, his face turned always toward emptiness; he doesn't laugh or cry, only his lip muscles twitch when he's hurt by taunts about his phantom wife and child—awaiting the return of a 10 year old boy. Behind his eyes lies a hollow ringed by horrors only an empty face can hold at bay.

> The name, twibo, is also given to the pearly-spotted owl, a small owl of odd behavior; it whistles and is active

by day as well as night. Children chase it away from camps by throwing sticks at it, anything they can get their hands on.

Haruva, Timo's sister, her Rheinland legacy now made of many colors red yellow blue purple pink lilac printed flowers all sewn together fourteen yards full of survived identity on display never grey anymore duku reshaped to visualize horns of ancestral cattle as leather headdresses did before, pours tea for us and scolds the cruelty of the young men saying Twibo knows his work and behaves well and is therefore a good person like anyone else; stop it. They do, embarrassed; understanding the tragedy too well, still feeling the sting of dispossession with minds and bodies intact, their laughter covering impotency. . .

does she still hear her grandmothers submitting in sweating rooms kept bare and in order for the deutsche Leutnant by boys mission-trained in domestic service both women and men finding means of survival for their families

Karatja just now sewing her first long dress of womanhood carries in her womb Tjera's child although their families haven't completed marriage negotiations carries too the caucasian gene for lactose digestion doesn't suffer the diarrhea sign of abundance anticipated longed-for enjoyed when cows fill up again after rains begin everyone drinks cups full of fresh uncultured milk and runs to the bush for a couple days clearly there's a white man back there somewhere . . . it's not likely that gene was welcomed voluntarily no one willing to talk about that insisting her ancestry is all Mbanderu now as then no doubt accepting the child as fully kin . . . tied through the living to thousands killed after hearing the gospel survivors compressed into creating a new identity—blood carrying invisible signs of a subjugation undeniably demonstrated by command of private bodies. Authority advertised by amusement.[81]

In Tsau at the turn of this century Tawana rulers sometimes forced Zhu to copulate in public consummating
their recently consolidated links in the colonial chain.

Twibo stands, balances a bucket on his head, silently goes with
two girls balancing buckets on their heads to bring more water
from the well. He knows his work and behaves well and is therefore a good person like anyone else.

Reading the ground

Out with Ninnow—reading spoor, not hunting now; too early in the year for setting snares, sand still too wet, grass too thick. And he's lost the stamina for active hunting—stalking, running. One of the most successful gardeners here; gave me six green mealies yesterday—two would have been enough for me alone, but not enough to share at my fire. . .

Glin stops by every morning usually with Tasa—sometimes I wish they wouldn't, sometimes the thought that things should have been otherwise is too strong   she feels it too tells me her second daughter Ssao's daughter announced by a call through the wall behind which she was born just beginning to stand alone reaching for my coffee cup ignoring the one I've given her mother will be my wife. . .

> the child was asleep I'm sure didn't reach for the bottle of wine I gave Ssao when he returned near midnight from the rainpool cattlepost at Tinagu to ask people there to come in for blood sampling today Damo and John made feeble excuses too lazy I was preoccupied with writing would have gone if a horse had been available but only donkeys were around dusk Ssao said he's go even though Glin was alone her husband away he wanted one of their few nights together I knew the wine would bridge several gaps. . .

but those are wistful days, infrequent. . .

> had been back a month preoccupied with getting a new camp set up new research underway absorbing the change that had occurred here the changes within myself Ninnow appeared one evening at first dark when I was alone said he had no time for a cup of coffee underscoring my feeling that

he had avoided me for the past several days letting his absence speak to me but I put it off

> when are we going out   let's go to where we got the
> two duikers

it was he who helped me work out the procedure for counting
spoor patiently teaching me along with Zona and Ssao and Tase
and Hum and Maitso to distinguish |u from ǂau critical to know
the difference between steenbok and duiker as well as the other
buck animals in words and hoofprints.

Ninnow gave Carl his name, thus became his name-grandfather
and my classificatory father. Later, when Lisa arrived, I wanted
her to be called Nisa, finding aesthetic satisfaction in the symetry
of the names. But she is Carl's sister and my daughter and the
logic of kinship overrode rhyme so her name is Bau the name of
Ninnow's aunt.

As we were leaving this morning, Lisa's name-cousin's mother, Ninnow's brother's wife, called

> Bau-father where are you going with your father
> Ninnow

> Kwidum; where we got the duikers.

> bring nnozwa to me   moon will take me soon

these goddamn counts have to go on without them I'd have only
another story anecdote not data all the tedious hours of walking
with eyes glued to the ground would be wasted actually it's no
more tedious than hunting even the initially exciting seconds surrounding a kill become routine through repetition leaving plenty
of time to look around inside my head

> this is where you found me years ago   my camp was
> here

Jerked out of dreams. . .

> Ee, years ago, I know this place. . .

He lived on this spot with a large group in 1973, 12–14 huts, more than 50 people; we started our journeys here—hunting, spoor counts, he showing me things; the camp split in 1975 over an argument about land rights and the digging of a well—at about this season, a little later, mealies had been harvested; he was snaring guineas in the thorn brush fence around the abandoned field: he began building a new camp and I got thirteen birds, one each on thirteen consecutive days; while the new camp was constructed we made our regular trips—coming back from these I noticed a wide swath being cut between the old and new camps and was told it would make moving easier. . .

> New camp looks good. When will you move?
>
> perhaps tomorrow   perhaps you can bring the truck
> just after sunup

Things fell immediately into place: thirteen birds and two-weeks' road clearing could be redeemed by hauling a camp to a new location.

> Just after sunup. I'll come to you. . .

He isn't interested in counting tracks today, just wants to be out together enjoying what we have enjoyed for six years; he hadn't wanted to ask if these times were at an end—lets me do the reading, tapping with his stick those few spoor I overlook, correcting my infrequent errors.

> Small ones, steenbok and duiker, are pairing again
> after staying separate during last year's dryness; there
> are many young.
>
> uhn   there will be many now
>
> What's this? Doesn't look like leopard; maybe I forget.
>
> cheetah
>
> Cheetah? The one with spots like a leopard?

I ask to be certain: k!ao, !ao, and ‖ao can sound alike in the wind (cheetah, hyaena, ratel); no more than vein and vagina really, nor than fun and sun in English. Yet—cheetah are rare; I've never seen its spoor before and only one in the flesh, that a glimpse in a game reserve. I don't count that.

Following an animal's spoor you enter unobtrusively into its private life for a moment; accumulate such moments, many repetitions, many conditions, piece together individual behaviors; learn a species. Seeing where this cheetah stopped to scratch, where it inspected an empty hole in the side of a termite hill (remember the tenants of other holes, what the cheetah was looking for), where it lay down under a terminalia bush—entering its space for a short time; the animal's image as real a presence as if its body were here. . .

we once followed a pair of jackal spoor to the point where they killed a steenbok Ninnow told me that long ago he had seen where a lone jackal had killed a kudu fawn so he knew that was possible but seldom happened at Dobe in September 79 Maswe and I saw where a lion cub had killed a hare dragged it under an acacia disemboweled it and buried the entrails before eating. . .

a common habit of lions which Zhu know routinely from reading the ground. They aren't the only people who know such things, Mbanderu can read spoor as well as any Zhu. . .

Tjitjo's saddled donkey slipped away one moonless night talking we didn't hear it go with a flashlight he followed its spoor through those of dozens of other donkeys goats cattle and brought it back. . .

women as well as men, too: more than once Shea corrected Zona when we were out together. Batswana who live on the ground know the ground. Nineteenth century European hunters knew such things; they lived close to their guides and drivers: not for egalitarian reasons, they were above all masters—

> Now, when a savage, obstinate and stolid as an ox, scowls
> sullenly from under his eyebrows . . . it is about time to
> know who is master.[82]

—here for pleasure and profit (ostrich feathers sold for $1000 a pound in 1860 London).

For those living on the ground, reading the ground is one of the conditions of life, just as reading the morning paper is in the city. How else learn that duiker and porcupine eat the roots of tchwetchweha,[83] and therefore—since duiker knows things not known to other animals and does not fall prey to snares as often as does steenbok and since porcupine transforms food into fat better than all others except eland—tchwetchweha must have special properties, thus becomes an important ingredient in learning to diagnose and cure illness, to wrestle with god and thus help control the world. . .

> Early November 73: Ninnow came to me one morning at sunup
>
>> let's go
>>
>> I told Kumsa I'd go with him today.
>>
>> come with me. . .
>
> to an ostrich nest he found the day before the male rising from the nest and running at our approach we took half the eggs and left seven using one as bait in a snare but three days later the birds had not returned so we took the rest of the eggs and ate a lot of omelettes. . .
>
>> Don't forget nnozwa. Twa will have menstrual pain.
>>
>> haven't forgotten   haven't seen any

A few minutes later he veers off onto another path toward home, to see if the plant is growing along this way. He's slowing down—we used to return as fast as going out—getting old, 56 this year; the scars of TB and malaria must tug at him. I'll have to bring Carl back to see his grandfather soon.

Sometimes alone

I'm not always sure whether it's the pale light seeping through the sky or the cackling of francolin cocks—louder, harsher than more distant roosters—that first wakes me when I'm alone in my camp—then doves, hornbills; all the avian racket of desert dawns (there'll be dispute about this—not all deserts have so many birds, not all parts of this desert. Not everyone remembers the same things): rolling out of blankets, knocking shoes together to shake out scorpions (only one in how-many-hundred mornings?); fire going before the sun appears. I like to be well into a cup of coffee before Ssao John Damo arrive, the kettle continuing to boil for them, each hunkering down with a cup in turn; on leisurely mornings when nothing is planned we may drink three maybe four cups each, half-liter cups, while we talk, later catch up with neglected housekeeping while we decide how to spend the day.

Different waking in their camps: same background sounds, but legs entwined with others ringing the fire, blankets laid across shoulders, even in summer, waiting for the sun and water to boil.

Different in bush camps: usually no coffee although I'm expected to bring enough for the first day or two. Same sounds, same fire, same blankets waiting for the sun; repeating, probably for the thousandth time, certainly ten times this morning, the trivia that reminds the group it belongs together. . .

December 1979 at Twihaba beginning to move in the morning Tase calls to the others

> see you all   see that bush there   that's where we Twi
> and i saw the female leopard spoor   it lay down in the
> night under this branch just here and looked at us   then

> it went off along this way   Twi saw it in the night but i
> was asleep
>
> Aie, see me! Do you know why he was asleep and me not?
>
> sure truly   i'll tell them   i took his second blanket so he
> had only one and was cold

Shifting between trivias; reminded how some came into being . . .

> *saw David's new wife for the first time at the August feast in*
> *Santa Clara where we all gathered after my second long stay at*
> *CaeCae kissed her on the cheek from behind and nearly got*
> *slapped but David attracted from the dance turned to intro-*
> *duce us and the other time Rick introduced me to Mary at the*
> *hot springs in the Jemez she made me go look at Basketmaker*
> *ruins while she undressed in front of a dozen nude bathers only*
> *when she was safely in the water could I join them although we*
> *teased about the limits of embarrassment we observed them not*
> *yet entwined. . .*

How often we are told that natives—that is, people not us—
either go naked or carefully hide their genitals, as if it were the
severest sin to be exposed. We are so seldom natives.

It is true, of course; "natives" are careful in the camps of the
tellers who stay alone, who are known to be observers; where it
is also true that people do not fart except in rare virtuoso per-
formances such as Zona's. But not true where legs and trivia are
familiar. . .

Shifting her legs as she tends her fire

> you see Twi   you see my gxum gets exposed   what
> can i do   i don't have panties   bring me panties   blue
> ones. . .

The very English aunt of a friend told us around a dinner table
that she had remained a widow for half-a-century because she
couldn't face relearning all that intimacy of living together.

Different too in camps on the road: camps set up in unknown places wherever night happens to fall; often I drive far into the dark.

Trucks are the most alien things here where nothing is made for them not even the track that must be followed, often forced through by sheer willpower; oxwagons were probably more comfortable——Livingstone said so, compared travel in them to pleasant Sunday outings——but then, he compared malaria to a mild case of flu. . .

asking directions knowing too well that the statement there is only one road is not given as assurance that we will find only a single track without branches but as factual information that only a single set of decisions will bring us past all the wrong turns to Tsodilo where none of us has been before taking two wrong turns but realizing our errors quickly after a few kilometers in the first case some inner orientation overriding Ssao's logical argument that bare footprints meant Zhu lived along that track consensus correcting the second where we found a deserted village and the four-year-old battery gave out in the heat its acid burning my right forearm from which skin sloughed off for weeks we had to dig trenches in the sand so we could push the Toyota to start the engine I jumped in at the moment I knew we could make it go no faster and we all knew then that the engine must not stall in the truly nightmarish sand we encountered in the last 28 kilometers not knowing if it would be 8 or 80 last kilometers because that sand is bottomless all of us tightjawed containing urgent bladders until we reached Tsodilo and found those we were to meet. . .

next evening I wanted to walk from our excavation across the hills to camp rather than ride around was told I'd find spoor at the top the tracks I found made by a hunting party that morning circling in search of specimens for the museum footprints becoming nonexistent over rocks the sun going down fast came upon fresh lion spoor beginning the night prowl with nothing except a white t-shirt no matches not wanting to spend the night in a treetop without my knife even having lent it to Damo that morning so he could convert a five-liter oil can into a cooking pot turned back taking a beeline course rather than the loop along which I had come because the sun was way below the hills maybe the horizon now came to a sheer rock face and had to go up to go around would take half-an-hour I'd be lost in the dark thinking of Carl's letter telling me his apprehension at starting college was like that he felt on a difficult pitch not knowing exactly what move to make next but confident of being warm in camp in the evening from the top of the last ridge saw the rock shelter we had been digging then followed the vehicle track in the pitch black not until I was nearly in camp did I hear my name called guns firing to guide me. . .

Preparing to leave, we discovered that the spare had not been fixed in Maun and would not hold air . . . at the beginning of this trip the clutch burned out and that's another long story which Ssao never tires of telling but which grows cold knots in our guts. . .

then, a few days later, returning to CaeCae which we had left a month earlier embarking on a two-week outing, the Toyota in great shape now with new battery and tires—but the same spare which we discovered had gone flat again not properly fixed at the garage in Maun; starting the evening fire at what was to be our last camp before reaching CaeCae, Ssao mumbled

tommorow i'm going to fuck alone

We all grunted agreement that if this kept up something was needed to break the tension, if only masturbation.

We have returned three times to Tsodilo; no trouble. The heavy sand turns out not to be nightmarish—merely tedious.

Tedious introspection; if indulged too long I don't see anything anymore, least of all myself. What appears instead projected on retina-screens—not seen, really—is an image compounded of aspirations, ambitions, weavings in and out of plots of time, statuses.

Yeats and whiskey and Hershey bars pulled me through Korea.

> Why do we honor those who fall on the field
> of battle. A man may show as great a
> courage by entering into the abyss of himself.[84]

It seemed so pithy then.

No longer: given that you fall into that pit, you've got to crawl out if you expect to see something else. . .

> *It was hard to do the first time, sitting there staring at strangers,*
> *trying to catch the tonal difference between my name and the*
> *word for dog — wrapping the scent-marked stink of the little*
> *that was familiar around me. . .*

protectively carried all kinds of useless freight the first time to CaeCae. . .

> *the staring wasn't a total loss; I was here to observe, after all:*
> *learned that kids don't suffer from nibbling at the cowshit their*
> *mothers knead into plaster (I knew that, of course, having eaten*
> *cowpies as a kid; memory misplaced). . .*

had this great Swiss stuff to put in the water and wait half-an-hour after which I could drink all the cowshit I wanted

> *safely. . .*
> *while I learned words for water and other things from Damo*
> *and grandfather, Tjitjo refilled the barrel every morning with-*
> *out adding Swisstuff, and eventually, I learned about that too*
> *and accepted the new status quo since it seemed as good as the*
> *old one*

Manuel told me — this was before the borehole was put in to serve the school and so provide fresh water for everyone — that every time he returned to CaeCae from wherever he had been

——Maun or his father in Namibia——he had a hard time getting past the smell of the water but after a while he no longer noticed.

The process follows me to America: familiars don't smell the same seen through an altered lens. I lose the connecting thread, pick up too easily a wrong affair that does neither me nor the woman any good, find I must redefine what beauty is.

A single spring

They never grow old,
those new crops of calves that appear every spring

when the creek runs full
and your dog muddies the bed.

As winter arrives,
they are taken to fatten in feedlots.

But some of them die before others.

There was a black one, with swellings under its eyes.

On the last day I saw you,
we knew it could not last the night.

You will find bones when you walk in the snow.

Lisa and I took the day bus from Maun to Francistown in the southern summer of 1975 there we caught the evening train to Bulawayo and changed to the night train for Victoria Falls where we watched baboons hang from branches over the precipice to reach choice objects of their current desire. The bus had a driver plus a crew of five whose job was to keep the short-wave radio blaring, collect fares, and load/unload limitless baggage tied down on the roof. This happened not only whenever whereever passengers got on/off but also at pee-stops (Driver, I need to pass water!) if someone wanted something out of a bag, while we sat around the ground drinking Groovy Cola brought along by traders to sell enroute. Five men were needed because hog-tied goats being taken to market needed to be lifted up, and on the return trip the traders' bags would be heavy with new stock for sale in Maun. The middle section of the driveshaft broke on the pot-holed rain-rutted "300-mile-nightmare-of-sand" about five hours into the nine hour trip—the crew cut a fairly straight mopane sapling thick as a strong man's arm which fitted into the u-joints and supported with another pole lashed across the chassis the stubs of its excised branches knocking against the bottom of the bus rolled us into Francistown just at dusk.

On the way back we spent a day shopping in Bulawayo. Katja and Stasja had given us money to buy hand-cranked portable Singer sewing machines and had said prices were lower there. In a bookshop I found Derek Marlowe's *A single summer with L.B.* We hid the Singers under the train seats behind our backpacks crammed with other orders of cloth cosmetics medicines and our own few things in order to evade customs and insisted on taking them into the bus at Francistown to spare them banging about on top, so I wasn't in a position to complain about the truck tire on the seat beside me. This trip took 28 hours: two blowouts, but most of the extra time passed in an unplanned night at Motsetse—or maybe it was planned . . . after the usual food stop there at the roadside cafe before the long night drive to Maun while we were reboarding one of the passengers—a policeman in uniform— said the bus definitely could not go on because a headlight was burned out so the crew unloaded the roof and went to stay in the village.

Unprepared for a night on the road—no sleeping bags, sewing machines to watch—Lisa and I began to read by flashlight:

> *In the summer of 1816, after a stop to inspect the field of Britain's recent victory at Waterloo, the poet of equally recent fame Lord Byron (L.B.) with his personal physician John Polidori went on to Geneva where they met Percy Shelley and his lover Mary Godwin with her stepsister Claire Clairmont L.B.'s current mistress newly pregnant by him; Byron at 28 was the elder,*

Polidori 20, Shelley nearing 24, Mary 18 already twice a mother (once bereaved), Claire at the end of her seventeenth year. They took adjacent houses on the lake—Byron (with Polly) the suitably grand Villa Diodati, the others a small maison next door.

Marlowe filled spaces between the dialogue of their dairies and letters—it was a stormy summer, not only in weather. The imperious poets disparaged marriage—Byron, just divorced, cynically. Shelley (he too a baron {et} but for the nuisance of his father still living), married but soon to be released by suicide to marry again (Mary), on atheistic grounds, baited Polidori's Catholic orthodoxy:

> *Ironic is it not, that it is the celibate who*
> *preaches the sanctity of marriage. I feel it is*
> *rather like a mole lecturing on the techniques*
> *of flying.*[85]

Far from celibate, however, Polidori was a handsome hit with women especially it seems actresses in the salons of Geneva, even that of Madame de Stael, but he badly miscalculated in confiding to his companions about his current conquest:

> *She is a Venus [whore], is she not?*
>
> *She is not my lord.*

Stunned by their callousness, when a dry spell persuaded the poets to follow Rousseau's lolita-muse and tour the lake "created in beauty . . . just for a Julie, or for a Claire,"[86] *and visit the intellectual highspots—Chillon, the houses of Gibbons and Voltaire—under the mountain, he bid them a long journey and parodied their refinement in his diary:*

> *I would not wish Mister S. to miss a thing, over-*
> *look a flower, ignore a stream.*

The present Claire—once aspired to the stage at Drury Lane —was, however, not L.B.'s muse but a convenient pitstop from whom to

> *fain take a little love [aka sex] (if pressed par-*
> *ticularly) by way of novelty*

left behind to rail at Polidori

> *even a mistress is paid, but at times I am not even*
> *that*

who replied that his doctor's eye had diagnosed her pregnancy and that she could not keep it secret long. She was beginning to feel the confines of her concubinage.

War *writes Mary in her Journal, but it is a cold war as yet, in which the opponents use cardboard swords as if to emphasize the kindergarten tactics* [87] *. . . confined in the gloomy salon the seekers of enlightenment begin to spit at each other as spitefully as the ceaseless rain, read phantasmagoria, discuss new discoveries in galvanism,* [88] *and use pens to escape in a contest to write the scariest story. The poets disparaged prose too, and soon withdrew to write lofty poems.* [89] *But Polidori wrote* The vampyre [90] *and Mary began* Frankenstein *while Claire composed caricatures of Albè (L.B.).* [91]

At first light the crew reported that the policeman had a nyatse —glossed as concubine but properly a mistress—in the village.

and he doesn't want
to have his fortune told. . .
. . . just wants love poems about himself and
If you won't write them will anybody
write them. [92]

She came up to me after a reading in a bookstore in Charlottesville two years later and said she would like to see more of my work and deep into that night we began to read and write to each other,

throwing ourselves into the dissolving-snow-new-crop spring of Virginia:

In darkness,
a crow caws;
together, we wait for an answer.

Unruffled by the silent response
the crow folds its head back
under its wing.

While I listen

to a far off dawn
where we followed deer paths through new-thawed
    woods
hoof-printed arrows pointing the way
to piles of droppings,
marking places
we said were ours.

I read a sapling's story to you
from its scars.
And told you that its buds, tensed
with spring upturned on twig ends,
were its breasts;

you believed me, then
asked about those buds browsed off by deer
and began to write your own story.

In darkness,
I get up to climb a rockface slick with rain.

Fast — sinuous country roads: I love the way you drive. . .

That single summer kept spinning around my head — multiple
reasons . . . one of memory:

                    . . . the glance
    Of melancholy is a fearful gift;
    What is it but the telescope of truth?
    Which strips the distance of its fantasies[93]

I was lucky to have had a string of fine teachers who fed a richer diet than just birds that never wert so those Byron lines stuck in my mind all these years fascinated by the prospect of stripping the distance of fantasy fabricating a boyish dream

> I'll sit
>
> and I'll sit
>
> and I'll watch;
>
> and maybe,
>
> someday,
>
> I'll see.

One of my closest friends shared, more fair to say led, my interest in poetry; we memorized odes to idolized objects—nightingales and such—wrote our own to girlfriends. But I relished more cummings's satire of Classics conceit

> (O to be a metope
> now that triglyph's here) [94]

that suited an aspiring architect so well.

Another: Marlowe wrote that Mary gave Percy a telescope for his birthday-by-the-lake to view Mont Blanc more clearly, and write his poem. You bet that opened my green eyes wide—Byron's metaphoric telescope was formed in Mary's-Shelley's material instrument focused on the mountain reflecting the politics of paradise [95]

> The everlasting universe of things
> Flows through the mind. . .
>
> . . . .
> . . . The secret strength of things
> Which governs thought. [96]

More immediate: Marlowe didn't raise my appreciation of the fearful gift of melancholy, truly not of the transcendent consciousness only to which such a gift could be given, but he crystalized a case of that Kuhnian critical mass that generates ideas— and sent me back to rereading that single summer's work of Mary

Byron Shelley, only later could I find Polidori. An inextricable interdigitation of shared places, episodes, perspectives on events — the lightning storm seen from different standpoints rendered unmistakably by each, geographies of rocks of water flowing and frozen, cuts from common reading, class dimensions—emerged demanding a fresh look at Eliot's *Quartets,* Durrell's *Alexandria,* Ford's *Parade's end* each atomizing a single nucleus in alternate fields of force. . .[97]

. . . mediating between my first question—how to make my experience intelligible to others—and the making of myths, breaking of myths:[98]

> *Mary subtitled her story* The modern Prometheus, *Byron retold the fire fable in his heroic-mode* Prometheus, *Shelley stretched the frame of* Prometheus unbound, *Polidori's* Vampyre *coagulates old myths into a virtual précis of* Frankenstein—*the primal man.*[99]

A more elemental common strand than storm and rock and bitching by the lakeshore weaves these works together: current theories on the origin of life and the significance of the fire myth were much discussed at Diodati as also the experiments of Galvani and Erasmus Darwin (grandfather of Charles). Electricity seemed that it might be the divine fire with which Prometheus animated the man he had molded of clay, thus be the physical manifestation of spiritual love. Polidori was as learned in the psychology as in the physiology of the day, Shelley well-versed in chemistry. *Frankenstein* draws from all this and recapitulates the development of aboriginal humankind, distilling yearnings for a return to natural life freed from industrializing urban chaos. Shelley in *Unbound* sought to break the chains that bind humankind to its self-made false divinities; Byron's *Prometheus* shifted the site of divinity

> Thy Godlike crime was to be kind,
>
> . . . .
>
> and strengthen Man with his own mind;
>
> . . . .

> Thou art a symbol and a sign
>> To Mortals of their fate and force;
> Like thee, Man is in part divine.[100]

They wrote in the infancy of modern science, but embryonically
—for a single moment—anthropologically. Stillborn: they all
returned to navel-gazing.

Now, updated anthropology:
Why should a deity wish to bring culture to mankind? So asks
Radin of his promethean *Trickster*—and responds: because he
cannot attain development in a void and so attempts to bring dif-
ferentiation into the world—and man must intervene because
he cannot permit a deity to develop without the possibility of his
own advancement. The gods are forced to begin as humankind
begins[101] . . .

and now the gods are dead, and we have Bushman—our very
own mythic all-dimensional [hu]man—to pick up the pieces Prometheus dropped and show us the way back to natural life.
Who'll be next?

> We can be Heroes
> just for one day
>
> .   .   .   .   .   .
>
> though nothing
> though nothing will keep us together
> we can beat them
> for ever and ever
>
> .   .   .   .   .   .
>
> we can be us
> just for one day
>
> .   .   .   .   .   .
>
> what d'ya say[102]

Alomar's lead driving through the coliseum-filled Bowie concert
betting shots of Jim Beam to see who could spot another grey-
head in the crowd. Being us. . .

just for one day—

but you don't want
to be fingered or forced, you have no desire to be
sucked or entered or caressed, by a specialist
or a cucumber [103]

working out her own problems, more traumatic than mine. . . .
sinuous, twisting country roads

. . . you've found someone
and don't it make my brown eyes blue [104]

> *On August first, Claire told Byron of their child; she was sent*
> *off to London with Mary and Shelley promising to care for her.*
> *Two weeks later, Polly was told to go. The child, Clara Allegra,*
> *died in April 1822 at the age of five in the Italian convent*
> *where Byron consigned her; Shelley drowned in July. The year*
> *before, Polidori killed himself, never recovered from the psy-*
> *chic wounds of that single summer. Byron, had four years as the*
> *cavalier servente (kept man — nyatse) of an Italian countess,*
> *then died in 1824 in Greece where he had gone to restore the*
> *Classic land. Mary lived to mid-century; Claire to 81, never*
> *another's lover (some say Shelly's), ever bitter.*

There is always wind on this part of the mountain.
The interstate sweeps past a massive scar cut from granite;
its face had been molded by weather.

Always there is a forty-foot load of pig iron groaning
up the last grade.
I have to get around,
before going down.

Just here,
where the road-pull threatens to throw me into nothing,
one detail cuts the remaining ground from me:
I see your match fail to light in its curled cover.

His trick;
you have not yet learned.

There is always wind on this part of the mountain.

Even when you are going too fast to see the grass bend.

Winds

Early morning; false dawn, wind not yet risen. The three young women of this camp—two sisters and their cousin's wife, herself a cousin—still sleeping on blankets laid out between hut and dead fire, sections of the cousin's three children scattered on the sand beyond the cover's edge. Kao and Kusha, up before light, already returning with the morning's milking. . .

> *I had been in CaeCae several weeks when I first saw Kao seven years ago. He rode into camp clothed in what we would call rags, dusted by many miles and days on the move—driving cattle to distant water holes that drought year—his saddle, many times mended, a collection of materials resembling a saddle only because it separated rider from horse. Kao, quiet, self-contained, his bearing eloquent of the inner confidence he carries, dignified his torn shirt and short pants, the only ones he owned. They exchanged a few words, Kusha and Kao, then he rode on to attend his horse. Kusha's eyes, her whole body though hardly moving, shone with pleasure in his return. . .*

The people of this camp, more so than most others, Kao's brothers and cousins, their wives and children—four generations—share this self-containment, confident in their lives and values. . .

Wind coming up now . . . first flutters on the flat water from the east as always with the sun no matter which way the wind will blow the rest of the day unless a storm is already working does the air sun-warmed in the east rise pulling a wind with it but then the wind would blow from the west or does it occur so far to the east that nearer cooler air falls to replace the warm or does the entire process take place at a distant point and. . .

it's one of
the things I don't want to know may not even be true may be
only memories of canoes a thing to have some early mornings
here or in a tent boiling coffee on a Primus after a ski run under
stars fading with the dawn following fox tracks to see where the
mouse was caught far out on the snow covered ice of Lake Michi-
gan islands stretch westward from Waugachance Point at the
entrance to Mackinaw blocked by great slabs of green ice piled
up when northwesters blow across the black water not noticeably
warmer than the ice watching otters belly-slide down the drifts
until the wind rises and they stand up suddenly heads turned
towards the smell and disappear. . .

A distant point. Sometimes I think I might as well be at one, any distant point: watching old Tishe, long widowed, tending his fire, setting a pot of dried meat to cook—moving through his space seven years ago, forty-five years ago when he was first married, wearing combat boots now and cast-off fatigues to cover his shredded shorts instead of a bikini-like brief made from a steenbok skin such as he would have worn somewhere in the past.

Army surplus; like any other, the South African army discards its surplus. . .

Good morning, Mr. Gensewiese, I need to take some blood
from you this morning; as if he didn't know, as if he hadn't
been in this same hospital—different beds, different wards—
ever since whatever blew off his legs in Vietnam blew off his
legs. . .

Sometimes on blood sampling mornings here I think of summer two years ago vampiring the 5 to 9 A.M. shift at the VA hospital. It must be the brown fatigues that seem so out of place to me. They are brown; perhaps because there is a limited number of fatigue colors and one might as well be chosen as another, perhaps for better camouflage in the desert except this desert isn't brown.

Perhaps. It doesn't matter that extermination is no longer the order of the day, that quite the opposite is wanted for its labor, not even slavery in the nicely defined terms of international law, perhaps even something to be called independence in that same system—I can't escape the intentions of those intensely brown uniforms for which the skeletons of future scarecrows are thirsting.[105]

I can't be here in remote CaeCae without also being in its encompassing present. And past: iron artifacts lie more than a meter deep in the sand, cattle too, inferentially, although we haven't yet uncovered them quite so deep. This place has been remote only to those looking in from the outside; from inside, it has always maintained its connections. Long before the Portuguese 500 years ago touched the coastline of Angola and Namibia and with it the ancestors of the people here—perhaps collaterally removed but in contact nonetheless—the meter-deep metal and the cattle came down from central Africa, with or without herdsmen but with the knowledge of herding, along routes long in use for exchange of materials and mates, maybe sometimes given an added push by Arabs and much later Europeans compressing the waist of the continent at the equator, thereby intensifying the ancient right of the natives to raid each other's goods and services (Arabs and Europeans in their turn exercising that same right), some of them stepping aside now and then to relieve the pressure and thus move south . . . . . just as the Lakota were induced to leave their canoes in Minnesota and become the feared horse tipi Sioux Indians of the Plains and eighty years later be reduced to reservations . . . . . More recent ancestors, who lived right here at CaeCae, supplied ostrich feathers for the hats and fans of fin de siecle ladies at Victoria's and her cousin the Kaiser's courts—not to mention those of the wives of members of the Explorer's Club who, as late as 1968 in Washington DC, perhaps later, were required to use a side

entrance into the sacred precincts of discovery. All part of the
same world.

I don't think as these people do. NO!—I think just as they do and
about the same things, but from a different beginning. Sometimes
the atmosphere here almost shifts into another thickness—just a
moment ago, almost slipping into Tishe's space as if I were seeing from inside a Zhu skull into which no one had hammered
that people and ostrich and eland were once one with mixed-up
parts, that duiker eat certain things and not others and knowing
this helps explain the cosmos and makes catching them easier,
that in the absence of enough money and stores to spend it in it
is wise to take advantage of surplus fatigues and oversized combat boots into which dried cowshit has been packed under inner-
soles to make them fit, knowing how to make things fit in this
place having absorbed that knowledge into memories built inside
a skull; not having had to ask. When that happens—almost happens to me—the shortest distance between two points no longer
seems fully described by a straight line.

But the scene flips over while shifting and I remain in the audience watching the action on stage, trying to identify with the
characters. I know them well enough, embarrass some of the
younger people because I know their kin of five generations and
many side branches better than they—aware nevertheless that I
am not one of the actors, unable to elude the connotations of surplus fatigues that I bring from my beginnings in another place.

Yesterday evening, standing with Ssao on the slightly elevated
flank of the dune south of the wells:

CaeCae is beautiful now that the rains have come.

yes truly   CaeCae is a beautiful place   put a store there
a bank there   a clinic over by the school

That is not what I saw. I saw colors, forms, light—only incidentally trees, leaves and grass, sand, clouds: architectonics not architecture.[106]

But now, watching Tishe, I see that Ssao saw more clearly. It's all very well to dignify rags; they remain rags. Everyone sees that. Kao sees that and prefers whole cloth.

News of the human race

—I cannot feel myself God waits. He flies
nearer a kindly world.

       John Berryman [107]

Whole cloth . . . Why do we honor those who fall in battle, not
those who fall into the abyss of dead desires? Their dreams were
once as faithful, now no less annulled—you would think anyone
could see that, not only a displaced anthropologist still in the
throes of reentry into what a contentious world insists should be
his only country. . .

> sitting
> hands cupped with coffee waiting for a Greyhound—mind
> wandering who knows why to Cabeza de Vaca: I had done
> a massive paper on the early Spanish explorers for Ned
> Spicer in my first year at Arizona, and then last year found
> Haniel Long's *The marvelous adventure of* . . . in Exclusive
> Books in Hillbrow Johannesburg—Long suggests that de
> Vaca survived his eight year odyssey by strengthening his
> inner resources. Plausible. . .

Alvar Núñez Cabeza de Vaca certainly could see already 400 years
ago that all dreams were once faithful: shipwrecked on Galveston Island while searching for gold in 1528 he described what
he considered to be the savage bushman life of Carancua Indians
there eating shellfish peccaries deer pecans small-gold-colored-
persimmons. . .

> *I searched out climbed gorged on these Texas wild persimmons*
> *in the woods as a boy but never till later associated them with*
> *the large red ones from China*

. . . enslaved by the Indians, he called the island Malandanza Misfortune. When he got back to Spain eight years later, he wrote a report to the king and included items he labelled "news of the —— peoples" he encountered; he also expounded on the circumstance of his returning with empty dreams in contrast to Hernando de Soto, just back rich from robbing Incas in Peru:

> Although everyone wants what advantage may be gained
> from ambition and action, we see everywhere great in-
> equalities of fortune, brought about not by conduct but
> by accident, and not through anybody's fault . . . thus the
> deeds of one far exceed his expectation, while another
> can show no higher proof of purpose than his fruitless
> effort, and even the effort may go unnoticed. [108]

Cabeza de Vaca never found gold, but talked about it a lot — and opened roads for Coronado, Oñate, de Vargas, La Salle and a whole remuda [109] of missionaries. . .

> Squatting
> in that neglected part of town off center,
> its Deco prominence an oozing cannula
> in a wound composed of broken buildings
> only half destroyed,
> disused, or simply ignored:
>
> bus station,
> lineal descendent of those blockhouse forts
> chained across a virgin continent.
> Blockhead dreams of men
> set out to conquer worlds
> who find no gold
> but alternate reward
> converting native maidens into whores,
> mining alcoholic antecedents of bus station bums
> with whom they fill their forts.
>
> Bastions of security
> for those, only half destroyed,

whose pyrite fortunes have been counted,
and who, therefore, may be conveniently ignored:
heavy-bottomed men,
fissures at the corners of their lips,
eat midday meals of beans
and lick insides of their cans
as deeply as their tongues can reach;
porkfat women still roll
their hair in wired bristle webs.

Among them, Mennonites in near invisible illusion
move almost on another plane,
as grey mice in winter
burrow carefully through private tunnels,
sheltered under snow white bonnets.

Old heroic forts,
bus stations—
pinpoint magnets on still uncharted maps.

In another corner,
a single pair cling to last moments of each other
whispering—just a little louder than is needed—
final pledges of fidelity.

No one wants to hear.

Some of those promises will be remembered.
I think the fingers of a man
who lost his arms in combat with competing dreams
only slightly overestimate their number.

We are closer than we think to those faultless figures, empty cans
abandoned on the curb where they sit, almost among them—almost—it's in that almost where the problem exists: indifference
rendering a stark remove keeping hands comfortable cupped

around coffee behind temporary table territories inviolate across new stockades erected from inside of thin window panes, out there of the rhetoric of freedom gone wrong——

Almost among them . . . it's that almost that keeps some dreams empty, others full; each isolated in a solitary space solitary dreams somehow out of scale with the world we all inhabit all devoid of heroism.

Forget's father

A walking-stick climbs beside the door to the apartment in Gaborone. Moving slowly it makes its way upward as rain-swollen
streaks seep down the dusty wall; they are nearly the same color,
the streaks and the walking-stick, mottled; a foot or so to one
side and I may not have noticed it, it moves so slowly.

Trying to get through the door, arms overfull with stuffed grocery bags can't get the key in the lock—one of the paper bags is
dissolving, fibers slipping apart without tearing, like pulled cotton; if I'm lucky there'll be no glass in that bag, maybe get it into
the kitchen before it splits. They didn't hear my kick against the
door, the sound muffled by their argument at the far end of the
hall, by the bathroom it must be. So much needed to supply five
people coming into an apartment empty for months; a two-liter
wine bottle pours less than a cupful for each, no point buying
only one—for the tenth time, I hope I've brought everything;
the list had become a soggy blur. . .

> What do you want to eat, maybe chicken?
>
> unh   yah   young-chicken tender   not tough like
> korhaan
>
> get beans Twi   i like the way you cook beans with onions
> garlic pepper and those little leaves
>
> tomatoes   i haven't eaten tomatoes for so long. . .

Damo was with me in Gaborone in 1976; this is the first time for
the others. . .

> chisi
>
> toilet paper. . .

Kuse has discovered that toilet paper is better than sticks for wiping away pee. (I doubt it; smooth sticks are fine for the ass— anyway, she wants her own roll.) Whatever; I must have enough. What's going on in there? The storm will break in a minute— should take the walking-stick inside, exposed here; rain will hit it like rocks—impossible, juggling these disintegrating bags. I'll come back for it. It won't go far in a few seconds—its brain in the point of a head at the sharpened end of its pencil body, no wonder it moves so slowly; hasn't reached the door handle. There's time. . .

yesterday arrived in the heightened spirits of newness for some anticipation of pleasure of showing for others let's do something before dinner eat later at the hotel I'll see if Irene can join us at the reservoir Gaborone's water first the sun on its silent stillness watched a pair of pied kingfishers hover and plunge bringing up a minnow one time in five is that significant about the same success rate as Zhu hunters and hyenas in Ngorongoro and wolves on Isle Royale then the blue-black storm blowing in whipping up waves stinging our skins with waterneedles Damo calling come here Twi come here where is Maun there in the direction we came north Ssao pointing south. . .

> *away from the rainpool at Ggo filled with a goulash of mud and chunks of cowshit where last year at this time I propelled myself submerged hands walking the bottom only nose and eyes and forehead too I suppose exposed but I didn't need my brain then almost in touching distance of the great white stork feeding ducks circling uncertainly on the surface. . .*

Twi Twi see   those two John and Damo   Ssao was in that big bucket for bathing   they went in there in that room   they wanted to pour cold water on him   you know you slip around in that bucket   i had to stay with Ssao so i could keep them out

So that's what it's about.

>Come help me; this stuff is falling.

>you forgot tobacco

>Aie, I'm shit; I kept saying to myself. . .

Laughing.

>you're forget's father   you forget everything

Laughing.

>didn't you write it   you can't even remember what you
>write

>Yes—but the rain. . .

>just like Taa Hunchback   you know him   he forgets
>everything   one time he was out hunting and went to
>sleep and got back to camp without his bow-arrows-
>quiver   his wife asked him where he had been and
>went out and found them but they had come all apart
>in the rain

So much is forgotten:

>if i could write like you   Zhu are forgetting what they
>used to know   Herero are forgetting   you write good
>things   know a lot just like we do but you can't learn
>everything   somebody has to learn to write   i want to
>learn to write

>i want to learn to write

John, Damo; Ssao nods but, over 50, does not think of writing.

>i don't remember my mother's father   he died when
>i was still a short child sucking my mother   perhaps i
>heard my mother or my grandmother say his name   i
>think so   i forget   perhaps my older sister knows

I don't remember my mother's father, have seen only a single photograph of him taken in an Amoy China street; he died two decades before I was born on a tramp freighter of which he was captain—all he could get after the Great War, after owning his own vessals before—sewn into a canvas shroud, slipped into the South China Sea. I know little else about him. . .

> *Berlin spectra glitter through prisms on grey stone cobbles, raindrops, small cataract washing out reflections from street-lamps, cars passing; shimmering—I'm told by his eldest daughter, my aunt, more than half a decade older than this century, that he was strict with his six children, was more than two meters tall, had a massive red beard. . .*

I'm not certain of my mother's mother's name; can't recall hearing the names of my father's parents, but without having been there I remember the taste of persimmons in China.

Twi see me   yesterday you came back from east   Ninnow told me you had been at Gona

Yes, I stayed there three days.

Ninnow said you told him someone died there named Toma

Uhn, that's true. I saw it, ate goat and mealie meal.

which Toma

Ninnow's father's older-brother's son.

did he live at Gona in Mhapa's camp

Yes, in the house at the end.

that one at the farthest end   the last one

Uhn.

what   why didn't you tell me   he was my cousin too
see me   my cousin   i want to know about my people
he was my father's father's younger-brother's son's son
you shouldn't forget people   why didn't you tell me

Buy me this

God eats corpses; that's what they are for. Why else would people die? Kamko painted a picture of god—in his administrator manifestation, equated now with Satana, our devil—cooking corpses in a giant iron pot, the kind of three-legged pot, small ones, in daily use by every CaeCae family, every rural family throughout southern Africa—large ones used in feasts and school lunch programs. The kind of pot, giant ones, depicted in cartoons of cannibals cooking missionaries.

When there are not enough corpses, god eats flies.

During the time when things were being created—in the beginning of time—everything ate everything else, metonymically exchanging parts as species sorted themselves out: people lost body hair and feathers, lost horns and hooves and scales; snakes lost limbs; ostrich gained feathers and eland cloven hooves. As each species was finished, it ate only the food appropriate to it and was no longer transformed. . .

> *Kao told me that the first time he saw the hairy chest of a shirt-*
> *less white man he thought to himself: yao   isn't he finished*

Transformations never cease.

Twi buy me candy
Twi buy me Groovy Cola
buy me a shirt
buy me pants

Getting silly

buy me a tow
buy me a big-ice-can (liquid nitrogen tank)

Usually led by Tishema, who also has my name is often called
Edema, Little-Ed: bunches of kids run around me lying prostrate
on the sand hiding from insufferable heat in the shifting shade of
my kitchen tree; they dart back and forth, taking turns shouting
mock demands, mimicking the constant begging of their parents
in hard times. . .

> see   you know Old Dun
> saying give me mouli
>   give me mouli
> all the time saying that
> all the time   give me mouli

All these kids have shirts and pants now, only one each and those
torn after a few weeks wear—Glo won't go to school because
his shirt and pants are more like strings than cloth—but all have
more mealie meal than they want; their parents have told me not
to bring that stuff for Christmas—hard for me to imagine, until
now mealie meal was, after meat, the most prized food, the most
necessary food for a feast.

> don't bring mouli   bring samp [hominy]

When I manage to grab a careless ankle saying I'm going to eat
them all, that I eat the blood I take from their parents, they run
away squealing in horror leaving their playmate thrashing sand.

> where's the mouli   give me mouli

Tasa begins to call out any time she sees me—tiny, apparently
frail (only 35 kg/77 lbs) but tough as nails, carrying her fifth child
on her hip—saying "give me food mealie meal   i'm dying of
hunger" with a sackful on her head, unable to suppress a grin all
over her face and finally breaking down altogether when I carefully pick up a pinch of sand and sprinkle it in her hand saying
"that's your mouli for today"; daily variations, twice daily, more
—vying for temporary advantage in our joke she has acquired
the nickname Mouli: Tasamouli. . .

but she hasn't always joked about food was among the most avid
diggers in kraal cowshit-carpets searching for fat grubs which

when roasted are like little bags of grease not eaten now except for one or two dug out in spring more for nostalgic value than appetite the way I have often revived Old Texas with pork melts really liking that kind of trash though it reminds me of lean times. . .

> dogs don't eat Khum answered when I asked about the paper-thin dog lying past hunger in his camp you get a first approximation of the food supply by looking at the dogs when there are no dogs things are really bad

April 1980: they can play in this way now, taunting the distant hunger they do not feel; women 10% heavier than ever before, stomachs satisfied, wombs overfull. But hunger isn't that distant. Just last September the accumulated richness of four good rain years was used up, all staple crops—wild and sown—had failed, cows were dry; people were eating resin by the handful to placate shrinking stomachs—equivalent to living on pine gum. Then drought relief was added to the small school lunch program, and aid to dependents: bags printed with redwhiteandblue shields and clasping white/black hands and Gift of the American People became the main source of cigarette paper, another item always in short supply here. Fat-time arrived. But not a solution to the continuing problem: dimensions of that problem perceived four years ago—more years ago, but spoken to me then. . .

> when the borehole is put in there will be no jobs   we
> won't have to lift water from the wells   cattleowners
> will have no need to hire us   there will be no jobs   what
> will we do

Dream of schools transport hospitals roads—fantasy facing fantasy dream of the future pitted against one longing for the past. . .

> I said iguanas lay their eggs . . . It is the process. They
> (or else the frogs) in the silence of the carboniferous age
> made the first sound
> sang the first love song here on earth
> sang the first love song here beneath the moon
> it is the process.

The process started with the stars.

                      [. . . the eyes of all ancestors.]
         New relations of production: that too
is part of the process.[110]

Untenable to condemn in them a desire for what we will not abandon—schools transport hospitals roads; in spite of uncertainty where schools roads may lead. Look at your brother, white man, in the twentieth century not the nineteenth or B.C. And if you know something about the twentieth, tell your brother, tell his sister—in a way they can understand; don't think they will take your word for it. A word that has not been reliable in the past.

They don't buy your fantasy.

Tasa will dig again; drought relief will end. There will be too many years of too little rain, too few jobs for too many men and women, but kraal grubs won't taste the same to transformed expectations.

Samgo's job

A high fence separates Botswana from Namibia: seventeen strands of barbed and smooth wire stretched taut across desert miles, hundreds of miles long; built in 1969 to replace an older, ordinary, four-strand fence. There's no doubt the fence helps control the spread of foot-and-mouth disease among cattle—elephants occasionally break down a short section; small diggers tunnel under and other animals—warthog, for instance—use the passage; steenbok and duiker dive between strands. There are turnstiles at the points where ancient footpaths-old wagon roads intersect the fenceline but these are seldom used, people finding it easier to follow duiker through the strands. But cattle seldom get through.

There's also no doubt the fence helps control movement between people. . .

> *April 76: Ssao and three others caught cutting the fence to get donkeys through after giraffe meat cached on the other side but they had hidden the meat well so were released after three weeks in jail for lack of evidence. . .*

April 1980: Herero from Makaukau drove 2,400 cattle 168 km to the fence cut through in a crazy attempt to join relatives in Namibia who of course could not help and were forced to return across the now drier 168 km losing many cattle along the way watered at CaeCae where they left foot-and-mouth disease where it had not been before

3 May: at Makaukau a Herero man called Badisa aside and spoke in Setswana for a long time saying he wanted the truth to be known about the drive

you Batswana dislike Herero   treat us badly

4 May: Makademai told me her version.

> Herero from the east drove cattle here   many cattle
> watered them here and cut the fence and drove them
> across into Namibia   two Herero men rode horses to
> Tshumkwe   when they got there white men asked them
> where they came from   and they told them from east
> at Makaukau and Makakun   the white men asked who
> said they could come here and they said nobody said we
> could come we just came with our cattle   but the Burusi
> called the police to drive the cattle back and now they
> have taken all the cattle back east   they thought the white
> men would help them   nobody is helping them

5 May: John rides up.

> i've just come from Nwama   many cattle have foot-and-
> mouth   their tongues are hanging out swollen hanging to
> the ground   cattle from east brought the disease   many are
> dead along the road   vultures are too full to finish the meat

The land still cut by the past, mentalities still tied to the lines: the
fence stands as more than an object. All outside power aimed at
controlling the lines while inside they say the lines are drawn wrong.

Everything seems so slippery; what may be true today is a lie
tomorrow. . .

> *April 75: Tohoperi, 74 at the time, his memory far longer than
> his years. . .*
>
> > *Ovambo killed my grandfather   how do i deal with
> > SWAPO   they're still killing*[111]

died at the end of March 1980, his question unresolved; although
we discussed it often he resisted my politics.

Not that his family never killed anybody; but put that aside.

> *My aunt said that my grandmother's death was due to inade-
> quate medical attention in the detention camp in India (but who*

knows what bitterness selected those words). We can't let the past
rule us.

Tohoperi resisted my politics because in reviving the past he was
asking how to slip into the present more securely—I told him it
can't be done that way. . .

In 1977, while I was in America, he mortgaged his large herd to
buy a brand new Toyota which he didn't need and couldn't drive.
When I returned in 79, it sat inoperable beside his kraal linked
visually now as well as usurally to the cattle that made it possible,
four tires flat, the battery dry, a clutch we would soon learn was
bad, a repossession order from the bank (when it stopped running, Tohoperi stopped paying). So I put it in shape and paid off
the bank in exchange for its use for a year, driving to Tsodilo and
other places while the transaction led to further reciprocity between us.

Not many Americans I know would think Samqo has a good job:
tracker in the South African army. . .

but when I ask the few Zhu I know who are in the army why they
want to fight they say they don't want to fight but anyhow sol-
diering is good and speak about a status they have not known
before and incomes higher than they thought possible and things
to send home to mothers sisters girls now in cotton print dresses
and handling equipment heretofore reserved for the hands of
Whites maybe some Blacks. . .

> *with animated glee Damo told of hunting kudu with a machine*
> *gun not knowing he was an anonymous element in the army*
> *hunting scandal that occupied the South African press for a*
> *while. . .*

and they asked if I had ever been in an army and when I had to
answer yes but I needed money for school adding that I know
better now they just sat looking at me

letting their silence speak.

Distances

Have you noticed?
Rugs thrown down from exotic distances
never feel at home,
and so they creep across the floor
with accordian undulations of a caterpillar

we return to places of our childhood,
where we know what will be waiting

granite deep.[112]

How do you deal with the price of oil?
Why believe in a Pope?

Questions asked in the evening, over drinks; to ask them one must know something about what happens in the oil market, what popes or preachers pronounce that ought not be believed.

a news item from Peking is as real
in the Finnish sauna as in New York[113]

But in the desert, foreign news—news without immediate meaning here, no connections—comes in strobe-like flashes too short to have dimension; it is impossible to know which part goes with which. America is wrong: in the desert you can't remember your name.[114]

January 74, at the gas pump in Maun:

Full-tank, Mma; and fill the 200 liter drum on the back. I'm going to Francistown—heading home.

no petrol without a permit

Permit? I didn't have a permit when I was here in September.

today you must have one rra   you must go to the District Commissioner

i can give you just 200 liters   petrol shortage

Petrol shortage?

that's all I know about it

It'll get me to Francistown.

Flight canceled?

no fuel   there's a seat to Lusaka tomorrow   you have a chance there

Flights to London grounded?

Arab oil embargo   we'll put you up at the Interconti-nental until we can get a plane in the air

why do prices for our beadwork fluctuate

what will government do about schools for our children

Questions asked at CaeCae are kin to those asked about oil and popes; often asked in the evening, over drinks.

Nisa: do the pills i hear about really work   will they stop me from having so many babies   i have Bay here and Toshe and Naaka and Kusema that little one has not yet seen two rain-seasons   and this one in my belly   see feel it right here   my back is killing me

Yes, they work. I'll get some for you when moon takes you again.

Ku: i've only got one   Kada here   i don't want another child now   there are too many people at CaeCae

Damo: let's have a girl first   then you take pills

We talked often—about how the pills work, that fertility resumes after they are discontinued. While the decision was under consideration, Ku became pregnant.

> Truka: Twi, look at me   i'm in school   i don't want to
> have a baby now   get pills for me ·
>
> John: don't be like me without school   stay in school
> take pills   you've got to learn

During the first six months of 1980, a team of government geologists camped at CaeCae in order to explore the surrounding country, "looking for any minerals" as they said. There were local rumors of oil—based not on information but on awareness of the new role of oil in their world. A world in which news of Augustino Neto's[115] death filtered into remote corners of the Kalahari not only by short-wave radio but more securely by word of mouth saying he was a good man.

Harara, Big Herero he is called: whose enormous hands carve the most graceful milk dippers and applique beadwork so delicately, served as a body-bearer in Hitler's War, on the British side:

> what is the biggest place you have seen

> I'm not sure. New York, or London maybe, perhaps Tokyo in a country called Japan. You have seen Johannesburg and Durban, know how many people stay there. Each of those places I named—New York, London, Tokyo—has more people than are between here and Johannesburg and all the way to Durban.
>
> we knew there must be big places   we had to carry so many bodies

Yet, 300 years ago, New York wasn't unlike CaeCae; cowpaths marked the routes that people took to wells and cornfields—later swoll up into streets without intention; retaining names like Water and Milk.

> *Still; it was a surprise, in these southern tropics near Capricorn,*
> *to see the Big Dipper rise upside down just above the northern*
> *horizon at ten in a March night.*

Often for weeks at a time I left my camp to live "just like them"
as far as satisfying external daily needs are concerned—sharing
the same pot, doing without when there was nothing in the
pot, getting what I needed—from string to sticks for toilet paper—from the bush. It is not a difficult life; there were times
when its virtues cast the defects of contemporary America into
sharp negative focus—at those times my sweat would stink
with apprehension, not wanting to think of the adjustments I
would have to make. . .

> *when I came to Kowri with the storm and dusk looking for help*
> *to dig me out of the four-day mud I was invited to stay the night*
> *in the hut of an old couple Kusaa and Decao we sat cross-legged*
> *beside a smokeless fire over which tea brewed quietly exchang-*
> *ing gossip taking the evening meal of clabbered milk they took*
> *spare sheets with a delicate floral print from a trunk made a bed*
> *for me on a cowhide mat their unobtrusive attentiveness that of*
> *gracious hosts anywhere a Chinese ink painting in motion spare*
> *economical brush strokes essential structure in place filled in by*
> *participants. . .*

But I did not always enjoy living like them. Often I would yearn
for a French goat cheese and crusty bread, espresso in a Cafe Para-
diso, a gallery, any film. My friends were aware of those times:
haunched around a fire, my mind would sometimes stray from a
conversation;

someone would say

he doesn't hear now   he is in his own place

They found that reasonable.

Return to beginnings

Zona's arrow, unlike Zeno's, often hits its mark, and I caught the tortoise despite its headstart.

Transformed images: projected through some geometry of perception to possibilities infinitely large, or vanished to nothingness where lines of visions cross.

Where does one focus?

> Marenga is reading the Sunday service from Mark 7:31–34. Verse 32 in *Etestamente* reads: Novo va eta ku je omundu omboro, nu ngua seta eraka, n'ave riheke, kutja a jambeke aka ku je; John's younger-brother passes his RSV to me so that I can translate—but not follow—more easily in English: And they brought him to a man who was deaf and had an impediment in his speech; and they besought him to lay his hand upon him.[116]

> But my eyes wander from the text nonetheless through the poles of the church where the cowshit has fallen away to the horse lying in its third day of dying taking some sort of note of its sporadic thrashing occasionally lifting its head not yet dead enough for vultures jackals the dogs having plenty this year so they can ignore what last year they would have killed each other to kill and devour.

> Our immediate intellectual ancestors were accustomed to speak of their neat and stuffy world as if it were an island of light in a sea of darkness.[117]

Reified in the library of Sartre's grandfather.

> Mr. Kurtz, he dead.

Not yet dead enough: Conrad's perception of disintegration in colonialism put into the prophetic mouth of a black savage; the savage not the one in darkness even though he had lost for that present—for all foreseeable futures it seemed at that time (notwithstanding that Conrad had told us the white man in Africa had died)—had lost the litany of his own destiny.

And for this present?

What possible futures?

The heart of darkness beats in blindness, not in African breasts.

The anthropology of our immediate intellectual ancestors is also dead although it continues its dying-horse twitch on the temple steps—

rejecting the conceptions of the people about themselves and their land;

> substituting semi-science, in that form in which western science is the most ethnocentric of the ethnosciences: hoping to prove that we can know about them more than they, unconverted, can ever know;

preferring to pledge continued allegiance in our twilit sanctuary;

> the sanctuary itself not indicted: close, inside, it has its own flawed brightness. I do not reject my own distillation of place and time and history, am sustained by those things I sometimes miss around a fire, and know which of the two places I will give up when that must be—and that will not be rejection; but to see what purrs behind lion eyes reflecting the fire it is necessary to pass beyond the hemisphere of sanctuary light. We have been shown reflections;

serving paradoxically as altar boys in a mass of self-substantiality;

> living Livingstone's legacy: neo-missionaries in the prep-
> aration of natives for our histories economies ideologies
> —counting them saved when they are recruited into
> one or the other set of histories economies ideologies
> (their choice limited in reality to guessing which carcass-
> half has the most fat); forgetting to ask them what they
> think of us, what they might perceive for themselves;[118]

continuing to serve god not mammon;

> it doesn't matter whose god, of Mark or Marx or JP Mor-
> gan: all gods divide to conquer, created to throw them
> that don't suck oursaviorass into the fire;

weaving the ethnographic curtain between us and them.[119]

I can not put aside childish ways

When I was a child, I thought as a child;
now that I am older . . . I think as a child.
I did not know that before.

Consider:
You must remember this, a kiss is [not] a kiss.[120]

Not only —

1. In 1757, a man, Damiens, was executed in Paris for having killed his father . . . after a full day of torture, "finally, he was quartered, this operation was very long because the horses used were not accustomed to drawing; the executioner was forced, in order to cut off the wretch's thighs, to sever the sinews and hack at the joints . . . the excessive pain made him utter horrible cries, as the damned in hell are supposed to cry out. The confessors returned and he said to them: 'Kiss me, gentlemen.' The parish priest of St. Paul's did not dare to."[121]

2. Jan's lips meet Maria's in a longing, lingering kiss, their silent haven from the words they feel unable to utter against the insistant announcement that his flight for Tegal is about to take off.

3. Georg's lips hold a still wet memory of Reinhardt's kiss as he waves goodbye beside the locomotive that had pulled the train from Budapest to Munich's head-in station, now left behind hissing impotent steam.

For Damiens and the priest who refused it, that kiss is a sign of pardon and eventual entry into heaven. For Jan and Maria, it is a sign of continuance, with erotic components sanctioned by a witnessing public. For Georg and Reinhardt, it is a pledge—not less erotic—tolerated these days but considered unnatural by much of that same public. For Bogart, who forever forsakes Bergman in occupied *Casablanca,* the unseen kiss (exchanged offscreen in a simpler past) about which Sam sings "As time goes by" is a measure of how great patriotic demands can be upon persons and how enobling it was deemed, in early World War II America, to subordinate self to cause.

A kiss, then, is more than just a private matter: it may be absolution, promise, stigma, propaganda, as well as many other things. It is a social form given meaning in individual personal actions. We label the surface phenomenon 'kiss' but do not see the surface alone; we see always below it to the context of its performance. And even such a strictly personal act is not performed unseen, if not by actual eyes, by tied down knowledge of what that act implies. Thus, to see even our lovers as themselves requires a thorough examination of our own subjectivity. An examination that can free us from subjugation while allowing us to remain members of society.

How much more, then, is the observation of another culture not performed unseen. Our understanding of other peoples lies not in themselves or in anything that they do but in our experience of them. Experience that is lived partly in their world and partly in a shell of our world that we wear when we meet them. And suddenly the picture is distorted.

We become the measure of those estranged lives and cannot listen to what they have to say. Unable to confront the subjugation of our own egos in our own historically constructed social setting, we rob them of their histories by subverting those histories to our own, constucting an empirical world that nowhere can be found.

Now that I am older, having gained age in Africa—it could as well have been in Bavaria, in Chicago, or . . . Guatemalan jungles could have furnished the green for those bound to that place—I think again as a child,

now without the wonder of childhood.

Ties

Dictated to the school teacher at CaeCae, given to someone hitching a ride on the first vehicle passing to Maun, from there routine air mail Gaborone—Johannesburg—New York—Boston; John's letter was waiting:

> Dear friend,
>
> Greetings to you my dear. I am very pleased to receive your letter on the 2/8/80. Even the camera you have sent I have seen it. The most thing is that I have no money so I am just waiting for you. If you send me some money I will go. And the Address of the school. My aim is to go but the main problem is to have no money.
>
> If you happen to send us money I and Damo you have to tell how much to each of us. If you try your best and send me the money soon, I will try my best and go there as soon as I receive the money. Damo also wishes to go with me.[122]
>
> Secondly I am telling you my sister's younger baby is ill. And my elder sister has delivered a baby.
> Yrs,
> John Marenga
> P.S. I have sent you an arm ring.

On my way to that letter:

> met Lisa in Rome to spend a month in Italy; saw in the Duomo of Sienna not a great Christian edifice but a pagan pit out of which Christianity crawled

in a Pennsylvania haven sought to ease reentry, one spoke of the drowned dead walking backwards all the colors of the sky in their blood—

> But hands grow cold with washing, cold as lava at
> night, cold that no blood can warm as they move,
> moving beneath the water, plunged down into the wa-
> ter or up into the sky where clouds sail with fish, and
> the drowned walk backwards through the streets to
> the sound of drum & bells on their ankles, like lepers,
> men who fell, lungs filling, all the colors of mountains
> & sky mixing in their blood, men & fish swaying gen-
> tly on the bottom, brothers in evolution . . . . . .[123]

by a mill pond in New Hampshire it seemed no loss to die mingling on the bottom with those colors drawn down

sliding under Texas CaeCae Brandberg cave painted Giant's Castle out of which it all crawled past Pleistocene pterodactyls sinking into oozing molecules bubbling as Venus now bubbles on its way to Earth when earth will be gone. . .

Do they mean anything?

The names? Not really.
It's something you should know.

CaeCae
Maun   Gaborone
Johannesburg   Durban   Cape Town
Bagnaregio   Laurbjerg
Ann Arbor
Dallas   London   Berlin   Boston
New York   New Hope   Newport
Charlottesville
Bayreuth   Villiprot   Berg
München   Chicago   Manchester   Berkeley
Edinburgh   Tomintoul
Austin

Sven Peter Birkerts

Janet Rodney   Gail Freimuth

Barbara Myerhoff   Vic & Edie Turner

Hartwig & Karin Isernhagen

Michael Hodge   Tom Frick   Anya Enos

Andra Birkerts   Grace Whittemore

Polly Wiessner

Manuel Nguvauva   Simon Tuvare

Ssao Kaishe   Dam Qam   John Marenga

Tony & Jill Traill   Irene Molebe

Trefor & Ada Jenkins   Jennifer Harris   Phillip Tobias

Hilton Ngwenya   David Dunn

Tom Huffman   Alec & Judy Campbell

Peter Sahlins   Jean Hay   Erika Albert

Karen Harbeck   Carol Kerven   Janis Diring   Ele Oettingen

Wulf Schievenhövel   Kathleen Stewart   Diana Blank

Martin Wobst   Annette Weiner   James Fernandez

Dell Hymes   Paul Friedrich   Eric Wolf

Roy Rappaport

Carmel Schrire   William Steiger

Duncan Miller   Pippa Skotnes

Die Trickstern

Marie-Hélène Perey   Jill Schennum

Richard Goodbody   JJJJ Denbow   Gregory Johnson

Jan Franksen   Monika Jacobs   Inez Franksen

Klaus Keuthmann   Ulla Gerlach-Keuthmann   Rainer Vossen

Pnina Motzafi-Haller

Johanna Schoss

Debra Spitulnik   Veit Erlmann   Rebecca Bryant

David Brent

Anne Griffiths

National Science Foundation
National Endowment for the Humanities
John Simon Guggenheim Memorial Foundation
Wenner-Gren Foundation for Anthropological Research
Social Science Research Council
University of Manchester
Deutscheforschungsgemeinschaft
Max Planck Institut-Seewiesen

Credits

Parts of the Prologue, "Sometimes alone," and "Winds" first appeared in "Passagen aus 'Journeys with flies — simultaneous biography in the Kalahari.'" *Trickster* 12/13 (1985): 20–28, translated by Werner Petermann.

"Entries," along with fragments of "Separate parts," "Rain," "Reading the ground," "Sometimes alone, "and "Samqo's job" first appeared in "from Journeys with Flies," in Thomas Frick, ed., *The sacred theory of the earth*, 199–219. Berkeley: North Atlantic Press, 1986.

Much of "Killer chill" is adapted from newspaper reports as follows: *Rand Daily Mail*, 1 July 1980; *New York Times*, 28 March 1981; *Village Voice*, 25–31 March 1981; *Washington Post*, 26 December 1980; *Real Paper*, 19 March 1981. It was first published as news clippings with my interlinear commentary in a chapbook of the same name (*Killer chill: poems for the South African peoples' struggle* [Boston: Boston University African Studies Center, 1985], 16–20), and translated into German by Werner Petermann as "Killerfrost" in *Trickster* 15 (1987): 4–10.

A much shorter version of "Return to beginnings" first appeared in I. Prattis, ed., *Reflections, the anthropological muse*, 40–41. American Anthropological Association, Special Publication, 1985.

I wrote "I can not put aside childish ways" in Munich in 1983 for Die Trickstern (Ralph Buss, Margarete Friedich, Ulrike Herle, Marie-José van der Loo, Werner Petermann, Ralph Thom); it appeared as "Ich kann die kindische Art nicht sein lassen" in *Trickster* 12–13 (1985): 20, translated by Werner Petermann.

Notes

1. A somewhat similar idea, a precursor in a sense, initially germinated in Japan when I was on R&R from Korea in 1955; I haunted book and woodblock-print shops where I discovered Hiroshige's *The fifty-three stations of the Tokaido road,* a chronicle in a set of prints of his journey from Tokyo to Kyoto in 1831, and bought one of the prints. This inspired the idea of writing a set of 100 pictures each with exactly 100 words that would be something like a landscape biography tracing my passage from childhood in Texas through to whenever I finished it. I wrote a half-dozen of these in Korea, but back in the States abandoned the project under the pressure of grad school. I began to think about it again in 1968, when on my first trip to Germany I found Albrecht Dürer's (1958) *Niederlandisches Reiseskizzenbuch,* his book of sketches and notes made on his trip through the Low Countries in 1520–21, and on my return Miner's (1969) newly translated *Japanese poetic diaries.*

2. In fact there are other witnesses: the people among whom I lived and worked from 1973 through 1980. But their voices are not available to readers of this text, and for me to interpret their opinions—as distinct from rendering some of their utterances—would be false witness. I had hoped to overcome this barrier by bringing my principal companions to live with me in America for a year, and in this context work with them on a companion text to *Land* and *Journeys* to be called something like *God eats flies* which would be an internal history of CaeCae from the perspective of people who live there. But circumstances did not allow me to do that. It cannot be done now: Ssao is dead from some affliction of age; Tjitjo died in the explosion of a gasoline drum; Dam has disappeared into the labor reserve; John remains in CaeCae.

3. Marks (1982: 9).

4. Shewey (1986: 16).

5. "Geographies" was written atop Kgali Hill overlooking the reservoir that supplies water to Gaborone, the capital of Botswana, in July 1977. Most of "A single spring" and the poems for my sons incorporated in "Songs my mother taught me" were written at the University of Virginia from February to May 1978. These were composed as independent pieces. *Journeys* began to form at CaeCae one morning in April 1979 when I wrote "A photograph of Heinrich Böll," the first piece consciously written for it. In addition to Böll, I was reading Borges's *The book of sand* (the first story of which is titled "The other"; my epigraph is from the fourth story "There are more things," 58), Jacoby's *Social amnesia* (my epigraph is found on 9), and George Seferis's *A poet's journal* of the hard postwar years; these brought my mind back to Hiroshige and

Dürer. Then, in the spring of 1981 Carl gave me a new edition of Basho's *Narrow road to a far province* (Britton 1980) for my birthday. The form of *Journeys* snapped into place.

6. David Brent and two anonymous reviewers pointed out flaws of form and expostulation in that assemblage; I am ever grateful to them for their careful and sympathetic, but cautionary, readings of that first effort.

7. Zhu is an unwritten language without an agreed upon orthography. It also contains many click consonents which are usually represented by the letters |, ǂ, ||, and !; except in a few cases where necessary to retain the sense of the text, I have changed these to their closest English sound equivalents so that readers will not falter over them. Otjiherero and Setswana have been written — in orthographies devised by missionaries — for more than a hundred years, nevertheless, I have greatly simplified the spelling of words in these languages as well.

8. I do not suggest that lions will never pounce on a sleeper beside a fire; they surely might. But they rarely do. One learns the parameters that control probability of attack — abundance of game, presence of cubs, lone old males; one can't do much about fiat or sheer chance — in the same way one learns the parameters that control probability of an air accident and assesses risk accordingly.

9. Chinua Achebe (1980). In speaking about the "factors that impede cultural dialogue between North and South, in this case Europe and Africa," Achebe says: "The fear is that the white man has found and used so many evasions to replace or simulate dialogue that he may go on doing it indefinitely. The first evasion is the phenomenon of the expert."

10. Roland Christ (1967: 22), after castigating Achebe for "ethnic reporting of ancient customs in conflict with new politics" and for "being long on native idiom and short on narrative interest" — and acting as one of the experts — says that is not "adequate stuff for novels, now that the anthropologists are doing the job so much better. . . . Perhaps no Nigerian, at the present stage of his culture and ours, can tell us what we need to know about that country in a way that is available to our understanding." Idiom and narrative are cast aside by Christ, who must, to survive, feed only on his own flesh, while Achebe offers a different sacrament. And I must face the fact that I am an anthropologist.

11. Elizabeth Hardwick (1979: 1): "One cannot help but think of a literal yesterday, of Idi Amin, the Ayatollah Khomeni, of the fate of Bhutto. These figures of an improbably and deranging transition . . . [of] a devastating lack of historical preparation . . . the anguish of whole countries and peoples unable to cope." To which Achebe (1980: 113) responds, "Would it, in the circumstances, be too difficult to wonder what 'devastating lack of historical preparation' created Hitler, Stalin, and Verwoerd; what 'deranging transition' formed the fate of Biko?" Or on a simpler scale, as we shall have occasion to ask, of John in a Johannesburg mine, or of Twibo?

12. Europeans have habitually referred to dispossessed Khoisan-speaking peoples as "Bushmen," by which is meant atavistic peoples whose devastating lack of historical

preparation has left them able to do nothing more than grub for roots and berries, and fall to the bottom of the cultural heap when approached by any other peoples. Correctives to this ahistorical view have engendered what some choose to call a Great Kalahari Debate in anthropology, but it is really a dreary distraction from what Achebe (1977: 782) identifies as "the desire — one might indeed say the need — in Western psychology to set Africa up as a foil to Europe . . . in comparison with which Europe's [and America's] own state of spiritual grace will be manifest."

Brian Eno, in "Backwater" (*Before and after science,* words and music: Brian Eno and Rhett Davies, Island Records, 1977), satirizes this Western obsession with a primitive imago: "Backwater, we're sailing at the edges of time / . . . / but if you study the logistics and heuristics of the mystics you will find that their minds rarely move in a line" — and with Talking Heads the the obsession with a primitive itself projected onto thinking animals: "they're living on nuts and berries / they ought to be more careful / they're setting a bad example" ("Animals," *Fear of Music,* words and music: David Byrne, produced by Brian Eno, Sire Records, New York, 1979). The second epigraph on the second halftitle page of this book is from Byrne and Eno, *Remain in light* (Sire Records, 1980).

Anyone interested in this "debate" will find it detailed in the pages of *Current Anthropology* from 1990 until today.

13. I first worked in Botswana from July 1973 through January 1974, all but three weeks of this time at CaeCae and its immediate surroundings. I returned in January 1975 and, after a month-long survey of the eastern Central Reserve, lived mainly at CaeCae until June 1976, making several brief trips to the western Ghanzi District. During the northern summer 1977 I analyzed collections in the National Museum, Gaborone. I went back to CaeCae in April 1979 and stayed until August 1980; this time I traveled widely and frequently to other parts of Botswana and South Africa in order to increase the size and diversity of my sample universe. Since then, I have worked in various parts of Botswana for some part of almost every year. During 1992–93 I taught in the Department of Social Anthropology at the University of the Witwatersrand in Johannesburg.

14. On my second day in CaeCae, Manuel Nguvauva, who had been away visiting at Magopa, returned—having been sent for to be my interpreter. He had completed sixth grade at Maun Secondary School and knew quite a bit of English. It was his presence that allowed me to understand what was happening here.

15. *Tow* is Zhu for "motor vehicle," from *mahowtow,* which is Otjiherero taken from "auto," with the noun prefix *ma* added.

16. The other two were Polly Wiessner, then a graduate student in anthropology at the University of Michigan, who studied gift-giving networks, and Dwight Read, a mathematician-anthropologist at UCLA interested in kinship.

17. I estimate that I walked about 12,000 kilometers during the course of my fieldwork between 1973 and 1980, perhaps 20 percent of that alone.

18. Zhu children are incorporated into their social group by being given the name

of one member of a specified set of same-sex relatives. A firstborn son usually receives the name of his paternal grandfather, a firstborn daughter that of her paternal grandmother; second-born children receive the names of maternal grandparents. Thereafter, parents' older siblings take precedence. The name-giver is called Big-Name of the name receiver, who is the Little-Name of that person. In English, these terms are usually glossed grandfather/grandmother and grandchild respectively. Zhu have a system of kinship extension called "universalizing" by anthropologists; that is, all persons with whom they have frequent contact, including anthropologists, are given a place in a Zhu kin network through the mechanism of being given a name. Such persons acquire, thereby, a namegiver-grandparent along with the kinship coterie of the name-giver and the obligations entailed.

19. In passages of dialogue, I follow current linguistic practice for Khoisan languages (Köhler 1989–97; Snyman 1975; Traill 1994) and use only lower case letters (except for names) and no punctuation for Zhu speech; I extend this to Mbanderu and Tswana speech to distinguish all three from my own.

20. The Arctic is littered with abandoned remains of searches for oil. In July 1961, I was a member of a four-man party excavating a site at the mouth of the Firth River in Yukon Territory for Scotty MacNeish. On one of our exploring trips, we found one of these abandoned camps and ransacked it for anything useful.

21. Mealie meal is corn meal that is ground fine and cooked as porridge; it is also called mouli.

22. *Molapo* is a Tswana word meaning "dry water course"; the plural is *melapo.*

23. A major focus of my studies was the relation of economic production to social reproduction. This involved investigation of nutritional status and fertility performance, as measured by such variables as cholesterol and estrogen in the blood of individuals. Blood was collected for this purpose.

24. Heinrich Böll (1976a: 34, 61).

25. Rick and David, born in 1953; Nancy, 1954; Carl, 1956; Lisa, born in 1958, had a crib in her parents' room.

26. T. S. Eliot (1952: 7).

27. NORAD, Norwegian Agency for Development Cooperation; *boerwors* is farmer sausage (Afrikaans).

28. *Kadi* is Zhu for a home-brewed beer, rather like hard cider.

29. *Goba* refers loosely to any non-Tswana Bantu-speaking person who lives around the Okavango Delta.

30. At the time, Rick used the name Sid Dillinger when recording his guitar tapes.

31. *Medila* (Setswana) is cultured milk similar to curds and whey.

32. Lieutenant-General Lothar von Trotha, commander-in-chief of the German army in South West Africa from June 1904 until November 1905. On 2 October 1904, he issued his Extermination Order (Vernichtungs Befehl), which reads in part: "The Herero people will have to leave the country. Otherwise I shall force them to do so by

means of guns. Within the German boundaries, every Herero, whether found armed or unarmed, with or without cattle, will be shot. I shall not accept any more women and children. I shall drive them back to their people — otherwise I shall order shots to be fired at them. These are my words to the Herero people. [Signed]: the Great General of the Mighty Kaiser, von Trotha."

It is estimated that 60,000 Herero, 10,000 Nama, and an unknown number of Zhu were killed in the so-called German-Herero War, the result of von Trotha's extermination order. Theodor Leutwein, Governor of German South West Africa from 1894 to 1904, opposed von Trotha's methods—"not because I am sentimental about the native population, but because I have our own cause in mind" (he foresaw the need for their labor). But policy reasons were not enough; he was replaced as governor by von Trotha in November 1904. Horst Dreschler's (1980) is the best scholarly synthesis of this period. There are other syntheses equally powerful, such as the reminiscence of a German soldier who participated in the slaughter: "The death-rattle of the dying and the shrieks of the mad echo in the sublime stillness of infinity" (*Die Kämpfer,* 1907: 214), and Pynchon's (1978: 261–73) fictional internal soliloquy of a German veteran of the Herero War: "The conclusion was irresistible: you were in no sense killing. The voluptuous feeling of safety, the delicious lassitude you went into the extermination with . . . a logic that chilled the comfortable perversity of the heart, that substituted capability for character, deliberate scheme for political Epiphany . . . the year after Jacob Marengo died." When I read that during a rain storm in CaeCae, I could not wait to ask John — whose surname is Marenga — if he had an ancestral relative named Jacob. He replied that he didn't know, we would have to ask his father, whose understated answer was for me the most powerful of all syntheses of that unequal conflict. I should add that Dreschler and Pynchon are speaking of a different man, not John's kinsman; Jacob Marenga was killed by Germans at Otjiheke in 1904, Jacob Marengo by British in 1907 near Upington, South Africa. It doesn't matter; the immediacy of that evocation of history in that setting tied past and present together for me as few other things could have done.

33. Sechele was chief of the Kwena branch of Batswana from 1829 to 1892; he was David Livingstone's only convert to Christianity — and that only temporary, Sechele being unwilling to relinquish three of his four wives. The quotation is from Leyland (1966: 134).

34. A telling recent example is this. Margaret Mead (1979: xi–xii) begins her foreword to *Namkwa: life among the Bushmen* by Hans-Joachim Heinz and Marshall Lee (it is Heinz's story; Lee is a ghost writer): "This book is a unique story of one of the more romantic episodes in the history of the encounters between a European scientist and a primitive people." Mead goes on: "They faced each other over thousands of years of technological change, and [Namkwa] was equal to him, just as their union demonstrated the extraordinary cross-fertility of all human groups, for she had borne him a child." Heinz's (1979: 37) own lurid language and his confession that Namkwa had

been "allocated" to him by broken men no longer able to find fixed values in their dislocated world are enough to shatter this sordid view of humanity. Achebe's *Things fall apart* (1959: 162) details the process: "Does the white man understand our custom? . . . He has put a knife in the things that held us together and we have fallen apart." The title of Achebe's book, from Yeats (1946: 184–85), "The second coming," identifies the characters: "Things fall apart; the centre cannot hold; / . . . / The best lack all conviction, while the worst / Are full of passionate intensity."

35. Wallace Stevens (1957: 77).

36. Cheese.

37. Jean Paul Sartre (1964).

38. English lyrics: Milton Leeds; music and Spanish lyrics: Alberto Dominguez. London: Peer International (BMI) (1939).

39. I called these lines "Shapes of flesh" when I wrote them for David in 1978.

40. Ground meat (i.e., hamburger) in a flour-milk gravy on toast.

41. Fifty cents. A quarter is two-bits; these terms were in common use then. My high school had a cheer: Two-bits, four-bits, six-bits, a dollar; all for Sunset better holler.

42. *Songs my mother taught me.* music: Antonin Dvorák; German lyrics: Adolf Heyduk (English version: Natalie Macferren). Two subsequent quoted passages, beginning "Seldom from her eyelids" and "Now I teach my children," are also from this source.

43. Wendell Willkie (1943).

44. The actual words are: "It's great to be alive / to work from 9 to 5" ("It's great to be alive." Lyrics: Johnny Mercer; music: Robert Emmett Dolan; sung by Jo Stafford (New York: Warner Chapel, 1949). Simply breaking the meter and rhyme was unmistakable satire, but there was a deeper irony, quite intended: the eight-hour, 9-to-5, white-collar working day included lunchtime, while we blue-collar workers had not only to start an hour earlier but also had to make up our half-hour lunch break at the end of the day. Not a few of our workmates resented that.

45. "Swinging on a star." Lyrics: Johnny Burke; music: Jimmy Van Heusen; sung by Bing Crosby (Dorsey Bros. Music, 1944). The end of that verse was, "And by the way if you hate to go to school / you may grow up to be a mule"; other possibilities were to be a pig (dirty), or a fish (devious).

46. June 19, the day the Emancipation Proclamation became effective in Texas.

47. José Luis Sert, a founder of CIAM (Congrès Internationaux de l'Architecture Moderne); The Architects Collaborative (TAC), the firm Gropius established with some of his Harvard Graduate School of Design students; Hideo Sasaki, landscape architect.

48. LaFarge took me into his Santa Fe home, there cleared my mind of many misconceptions, and illumined my path to the Navaho people. I also met another house guest, Ed Dozier, who had recently finished his Ph.D. in anthropology at Chicago; he later, at the University of Arizona, became a mentor to me.

49. One of my committee members knew Evon Vogt, Professor of Anthropology at Harvard, and arranged a meeting. During spring term 1958, Vogt gave me private tutorials in his office every Friday afternoon, arranged an unrestricted pass to the Peabody and Weidener libraries, and helped me set up a fieldwork interview program for my thesis on a town for the new helium plant at Shiprock.

50. I wrote these lines for Carl in the spring of 1978 while at the University of Virginia; I called them "Conversations."

51. I elaborate this idea in my introduction to *The politics of difference* (Wilmsen 1996).

52. Beckett (1959: 382), "The unnameable."

53. I decided to take the Ph.D. in anthropology because I couldn't find a job in the sort of social planning I had in mind. My teachers at MIT—Lewis Mumford, Laurence Kelso Frank, Charles Abrams—had convinced me that urban renewal would be the disaster it became, so that route was closed to me. Besides, I had what seemed a natural affinity for the concerns of anthropology. Consequently, during my first job as instructor in the School of Architecture at the University of Texas, I began to take formal anthropology courses. In 1960, I went to the University of Arizona still teaching architecture but as assistant professor at a considerably higher salary; there I integrated my studies with teaching until 1964 when I received an NSF Graduate Fellowship. Ed Dozier also came to Arizona in 1960 and we became fictive family; over six years of coffee, wine, and friendship around his kitchen table and mine he taught me the essence of being an anthropologist.

54. Anna Akhmatova, "Requiem" (1976: 23–32). Composed in the years 1935–40, the poem was first published in 1963. The quoted passage is from the section subtitled "The sentence" (p. 28) and records Akhmatova's reaction to her son's exile to Siberia during the Stalin Terror of the 1930s.

55. *Nie Blankes* is Afrikaans, meaning "non-whites."

56. This was first published as a poem "School's out" dedicated to Phillip Tobias in *Staffrider* (Wilmsen 1980).

57. In the fall of 1950, my sophomore year, the University of Texas (at Austin) was forced by a Supreme Court decision (Sweatt v. Painter) to integrate its law school after vigorous attempts to avoid such an action, including the establishment of a "separate but equal" law school at Prairie View, then the designated Black college of the state. Heman Sweatt was the person who persevered in bringing down this barrier; since 1986 the university has honored him with an annual Heman Sweatt Symposium on Civil Rights. One of the more shameful accomplishments of the Reagan-Bush "New World Order" is the 1996 decision in the Hopwood case by the Fifth Circuit Court (the same court that had been a bedrock in the desegregation struggle) which essentially overrides Sweatt and forbids affirmative action in admissions policy.

58. "Kaffir" is an Afrikaans word used to designate a native African, equivalent to "nigger"; the origin is Arabic *kafir,* "infidel." Chabula and other brands of sorghum beer

are packaged in the same kind of waxed cardboard cartons in which milk is sold in America. This and the previous paragraph were originally a poem "Let us go then" which I dedicated to Lorna Marshall on her 85th birthday; it is included in *Killer Chill* (Wilmsen 1985a: 10).

59. I wrote these lines as a poem called "False fronts" and dedicated it to Tony and Jill Traill, close friends and colleagues with whom I often stayed in Johannesburg at the time (first published in Wilmsen 1985a: 4).

60. I called these lines "A boy" (first published in Wilmsen 1985a: 6) and dedicated them to Janis Diring, my assistant at the time, who, despite her experience in public health in America, was so overwhelmed by the poverty of the people with whom we worked in the Kalahari and of those we saw on Johannesburg streets that she had to force herself to return to our work after a brief holiday in the lap of luxury on Mauritius.

61. Passbooks: in South Africa, every "Native" (that is, Black African) was required to carry a passbook during the apartheid era. In it were recorded tribal affiliation, assigned "home area," work permit, work history, and residence permit if in a White area. Passbooks were subject to police inspection at any time; persons without satisfactory papers could be transported to their "home area" and be required to stay there, even if they had never seen that place before. *Baas* is Afrikaans meaning "boss," the usual term of address then required of Blacks when addressing a White male. White women were addressed as "Madam," and children as "Baasi" and "Missie."

62. Williams (1967: 41) commenting on his writing *Kora in hell* (1957: 41) in which he, a medical doctor, observes: "The corpse of a man has no distinction from the corpse of an ox . . . Beautiful white corpse of night."

63. We sang "America the beautiful" quite often in school: "O beautiful for spacious skies / for amber waves of grain / for purple mountain majesty / above the fruited plain! / America!, America! / God shed his grace on thee, / and crown thy good with brotherhood / from sea to shining sea." The words were written in 1893 as a poem by Katherine Lee Bates, inspired by the view from Pike's Peak; the music was composed by Samuel Augustus Ward in 1882 and was then called "Materna." Words and music were first printed together in 1910.

64. "Columbia the gem of the ocean." Words and music: Thomas à Becket (1843).

65. "Edge of allegiance," *Timbuk 3.* Words and music: Pat MacDonald. Mambadadi Music (BMI), 1989.

66. Williams (1963: 83); the passage is found in Part III of Book Two, "Sunday in the park."

67. Soweto is South West Town, one of the satellite township locations where Black workers in Johannesburg were forced to live. On 16 July 1976, school children in Soweto boycotted the new law requiring that they be instructed in the Afrikaans language. More than 350 were killed by police.

68. The Second: on March 2, 1945, the combined Allied air force carried out a

saturation bombing raid on Cologne. I remember reading in the paper, at age 13, that the city's cathedral had been spared as a humanitarian gesture to our common cultural heritage—and wondering about the common heritage of the humans who had not been spared (no doubt influenced in this by my parents' often expressed worry about their sisters and friends in Germany). Böll, in *Group portrait with lady,* describes what it must have been like for some under the bombs. Ypsilanti, Michigan—named for a Greek general—was the site of the Ford Willow Run factory where B-17 bombers were built at ferocious speed in order to keep their appointment with the Second and other days. I remember when U.S. 12 was still the main route from Chicago through Detroit to Canada—this was in the 1950s, perhaps into the 1960s—the signs at the outskirts of the city said "Welcome to Ypsilanti—Bomber City."

69. Jane Sallade was a graduate student in archaeology at the University of Michigan with whom I worked closely during most of my ten years teaching there. We were devoted friends.

70. *Shro* is Zhu meaning "to strip" or "wipe away"; a Zhu curer uses his/her arms in a wiping motion to strip away sickness.

71. Kqo is the creator, called the Greater God by some anthropologists; he is now generally removed from active intervention in worldly affairs. Ganwa, sometimes called the Lesser God, administrates the present world, giving and taking life and fortune while causing daily events to take place.

72. Green mealies are green corn, young corn-on-the-cob.

73. Tobe is the end of the rain season corresponding to autumn, generally mid-March to mid-May. This is the season of ripening for most of the principal wild foods as well as for domestic crops. Large animals are most easily hunted at this time and cows produce much milk. It is the rich season. Guum is winter, more like Indian Summer, June–August.

74. Dogs ran freely when I was young; there were always many on any street. When a female was in heat, all males within scenting distance packed to follow her and fight for the right to mate; the one that won was called the *salty dog.* "Salty dog" is an old folk song that plays on this; I heard many versions.

75. In 1979, I donated five of Kamko's drawings to the National Art Gallery in Gaborone; these were subsequently exhibited in the annual art show, in which works from many artists in the country are entered to be judged. Kamko took first prize in drawing. In the same show, Katja took third prize in crafts for a set of her cloth dolls. CaeCae has done well in art competitions; the school chorus won the 1986 traditional music competition.

76. The Tsodilo Hills also have many paintings; at least one of these is of an eared or horned snake (see Wilmsen 1987). Kamko's first trip to Tsodilo was with me in October 1979.

77. "Masharo" is the Zhu and Herero rendition of "Marshall," specifically Laurence Marshall, who financed his family's expeditions to the Kalahari from 1951 to 1961.

"Norna" is Lorna Marshall, whose book, *The !Kung of Nyae Nyae,* is her account of their work in the region. "Jonni" is John Marshall, maker of a series of films on the life of several groups of San (see Wilmsen 1999).

78. Angelica-father: among Zhu, Mbanderu, and Tswana a person's principal identity is tied to family; thus, a parent is usually addressed by the name of his/her child (usually, but not exclusively, the eldest child) with the term mother or father attached as a suffix. In this case, Harara is the father of a girl named Angelica; consequently, he is called Angelica-father. In "Reading the Ground," I am addressed as Bau-father, because my daughter, Lisa, is named Bau. Kahai exaggerates the number of cattle belonging to him. The recorded count of animals killed is 108; Kahai here claims them all.

79. "Boer" is Afrikaans meaning "farmer," but the word is used generally to designate an Afrikaner person; Zhu and Herero pronounce this word Buru, plural Burusi.

80. This happened in 1957. John Marshall (1993: 31) says he actually intervened to help remove Mbanderu and their cattle; Lorna Marshall (1976: 60) says it was Lawrence "Mashaw" who motivated the police action.

81. All of the native peoples of southern Africa are to some degree lactose intolerant; most experience mild to severe gastric reactions and diarrhea when they drink fresh milk. This is due to a genetically transmitted variation in lactase enzyme synthesis different from that found in Europeans, who tolerate large amounts of lactose. In cultured milk—yogurt, curds and whey, cheese—lactose has been converted to lactic acid, and it is in this readily digested form that milk is usually consumed throughout southern Africa. During the early rain season—December, January—when cows begin to produce large quantities of milk after giving very little during the dry heat of September–November, many people celebrate their joy in the new abundance by overindulging, somewhat as some of us do in early summer when green fruits become available.

82. Thomas Baines (1968: 130).

83. A tree, *Mundularia sericia.*

84. I had three small books of poems with me in Korea (after the fighting: 1953–54), one of Yeats. I don't know what happened to the books. For years, I have attributed these lines to Yeats; apparently, he didn't write them. I now have a suspicion it was Frost. But I have lost interest in Frost, though not in Yeats. I may even not remember the lines correctly.

85. Page numbers of quotes from *A single summer* are as follows: 63, 172, 185, 172, 91.

86. Byron was reading Rousseau's *Julie, ou la nouvelle Héloïse,* which chronicles his infatuation with a young woman and a fantasy trip around the lake with her; the Claire here was Julie's cousin—there are numerous parallels to the *roman en scène* at Diodati (quoted in Marlowe, 136).

87. These are Marlowe's words, 229.

88. In the 1790s, Galvani had produced an electrical charge by chemical means

(hence, the galvanic battery). Almost immediately, speculations arose about the possibility of applying the technique to create life.

89. Byron to write Canto III of "Childe Herold" and "The prisoner of Chillon" as well as shorter poems, Shelley to write his "Hymn to intellectual beauty" and "Mont Blanc" and sketch out *Prometheus unbound*. Evidence exists for stories by Shelley and Claire, but these are lost; Byron did write a fragment which became the last stanzas of his poem "Mazeppa."

90. Published in 1819; this was, apparently, the first time the various strands of this old myth were brought together in prose form. The book was originally published anonymously (this was not uncommon then—*Frankenstein,* too, was so published and attributed at first to Percy, who wrote, and signed, an introduction). *Vampyre* was widely thought to be by Byron, who however flatly condemned this rumor—not on grounds of intellectual honesty so much as of intellectual arrogance—claiming such trash was beneath him (but Goethe thought it his best work!). Byron (1993: 37) was cruelly disdainful of Polidori's other writing efforts: "Dear Doctor: I have read your play, / which is a good one in its way,— / Purges the eye and moves the bowels, / And drenches handkerchiefs like towels / With tears . . ." —and so on for 91 lines. *Vampyre* was, however, vastly popular in England and France, was turned into a wildly successful play (Bishop 1991), and later was one inspiration for Bram Stoker's *Dracula* (Frayling 1991; Hindle 1992).

91. One example: "Imprimis to be a great pathetic poet. 1st. Prepare a small colony, then dispatch the mother by worrying and cruelty . . . thus a tolerable quantity of discontent & remorse being prepared give it vent on paper" (Stocking 1968: 183).

92. Gail Freimuth (1978).

93. "Dreams," Stanza VII (Byron 1933: 213–16).

94. e. e. cummings (1938: poem 138; unpaged). Those familiar with cummings's work will recognize my debt to him.

95. "The politics of paradise" is not my phrase, though I wish it were; I read it somewhere during my research stimulated by Marlowe, but I failed to note down where.

96. "Mont Blanc" (Shelley 1945: 532).

97. There were more ingredients to this spring of 1978. I was in the anthropology department at the University of Virginia during 1977–78 to help renovate the archaeology program. Vic Turner arrived at the same time—he and Edie were deep into their new work on pilgrimages; they hosted long weekends—some five days long— to which Barbara Myerhof, Bruce Kapfera, and others came from afar. We cooked meals, slept on floors or in the backyard, and all the while talked writing and read/ critiqued each others' works in progress. Roy Wagner was making superb translations of Rilke; Chris Crocker and David Sapir had just completed their *Social use of metaphor;* among my courses was one on the old BAE Native American texts—supplemented with reading, among others, Radin. I shared a pseudo-neo-antebellum colonnaded house with Hartwig and Karin Isernhagen, who were researching John

Dos Passos. It was a heady mix, constantly stirred—a structure for *Journeys* began to form.

98. To this point and from ". . . we can be heroes" to the end was written in Charlottesville in 1978. The intervening Prometheus section was worked out while I was a Simon Fellow in anthropology at the University of Manchester during 1994–95. At Manchester, I followed my usual habit of reading the works of local authors in their home settings; L.B. was the sixth Baron Byron of Rochdale, now a suburb of Manchester, which lies at the end of the canal by that name along which I would walk. I am indebted to M. K. Joseph (1969) and Timothy Webb (1995), whose words I have paraphrased here. On a trip to Edinburgh, I found Polidori's original *Vampyre* in the National Library of Scotland.

99. In the light shed by Marlowe, it also becomes clear that the tale recapitulates that single summer; L.B. is the model for the vampire, Claire for his victim (see also Rieger 1963; Bishop 1991; Macdonald 1991). Mary, however, gave him no credit for his role in forming *Frankenstein,* only saying condescendingly in her introduction to the 1831 edition: "Poor Polidori had some terrible idea. . . ." Shelley cuts him—and Claire —out altogether from his preface, saying there were, besides Mary, only two others (alluding to himself and Byron) in that single summer. For Polidori's contribution, see Rieger (1963, 1967).

100. "Prometheus" (Byron 1933: 191).

101. Radin (1956: 126).

102. "Heroes." Lyrics: David Bowie; music Brian Eno (Fleur Music Ltd. [BMI], 1977).

103. Freimuth (1978).

104. "Don't it Make My Brown Eyes Blue." Words and music: Richard Leigh; sung by Crystal Gayle (United Artists, 1976).

105. Günther Grass (1976: 206–207, 215, 579): "In a junkshop on Tagnetergasse he managed to scare up an old SA uniform dating back to the heroic period . . . those intensely brown uniforms for which he and the skeletons of future scarecrows were thirsting . . . SA uniforms . . . the togs of plain Party members. But everything was brown: not the brown of summer oxfords, not hazelnut-brown or witch-brown; no brown Africa . . . shit brown lay before Eddie Amsel, the Jew who survived by constructing true caricatures of his oppressors . . . for after all, and this should never be forgotten, the scarecrow was created in man's image."

106. However, I did try to help Ssao and the people of CaeCae further their vision. A borehole well was drilled at CaeCae in 1979 and proved to tap a strong aquafer of sweet water. The presense of such a secure source of water was a prerequisite for establishing a new school. Partly because of it, and partly because I was able to demonstrate to District Council the additional presense of a viable pupil population, a school was begun in 1980. I was also able to persuade Council that suitably skilled labor was present at CaeCae—several men had worked as brick-makers, masons, and concrete journeymen in Namibia—and Council agreed to use this labor under my supervision

(my architectural and construction experience useful here) as a means of boosting the local economy. Work began in April 1980 when a truck delivered 300 bags of cement, a brick-making device, and tools. Ssao and I were discussing what this might portend for CaeCae's future.

By the mid-1980s the school had been expanded to its planned six grades, a paramedic clinic was in operation, and a two-man police post was stationed in the village mini-center. Maka had inherited her father's Toyota and was running a successful itinerant small-trading business with Manuel as driver, but a permanent store could not be supported. And there was still no need for a bank.

107. *Homage to Mistress Bradstreet*, 35.

108. Covey (1961: 10, 25); Covey condensed de Vaca's subheadings "news of the ———" into the felicitous phrase "news of the human race," which I have appropriated as the title of this section. The original title in 1977 was "Fort Wayne," where it was written. It acquired the present title in July 1997 when David visited in Edinburgh and—in one of those conjunctions of transitive memory—brought along *La Relación;* I also made a few minor changes then.

109. Coronado retraced de Vaca's route in reverse, looking for El Dorado; Oñate followed him to found Santa Fe; de Vargas consolidated Spanish rule in the Southwest. La Salle briefly based his fleet on Galveston, thus giving Texas the second of its six flags. A remuda is a string of spare horses taken along on the trail by working cowboys so that fresh mounts would be available.

110. Ernesto Cardenal (1980: 20). The line in brackets is my addition, alluding to "the spirits of the dead—growing smaller through time until they disappear, reversing the process of life . . . their eyes the stars looking down on us" (see above, p. 41).

111. SWAPO, South West African People's Organization. Tohoperi makes the common mistake of identifying SWAPO exclusively with Ovambo interests although at the time a Herero was secretary of the organization.

112. I wrote this for Vic and Edie Turner at Thanksgiving 1977—after a fine turkey dinner and gallons of wine, Vic and Fred (their son) got into one of their famous arguments about peoples, places, encounters with these, writing about such; Edie and I stayed out of it. I found myself watching a small rug on their floor, of the kind called oriental, as it responded to rapid footfalls.

113. Hans Magnus Enzensberger (1968: 89): "The geographical centres of the poem, Prague and Lake Päijänne in Finland, are not presented as landscape pictures, but are stations in a comprehensive network of communications in which 'all distances are the same.' That is why the exploited countries of the world are included, and a news item from Peking is as real in the Finnish sauna as in New York."

114. The rock group, America, sings—in "A horse with no name" (words and music by Dewey Bunnell [Warner Bros., 1971])—"in the desert, you can remember your name / 'cause there ain't no one for to give you no pain," mistaking emptiness for insight, thereby missing the comprehensive network of communication.

115. A founder of MPLA and first president of independent Angola.

116. *Etestamente epe RaMuhona Jesus Kristus puna Omapsalme* (The New Testament of Jesus Christ and the Psalms). Pretoria: Nasionale Boekdrukkery Beperk, 1968.

117. Scott Buchanan (1975: 33).

118. Von Trotha, in his *Befehl* (see above, note 32), almost parodies Conrad's (1950: 81) irony in Marlow's (his?) reaction to an ivory station chain gang: "After all, I also was a part of the great cause of these high and just proceedings."

119. This was written at the end of 1980; as I noted in the prologue, ethnographic practice has changed significantly in the interim.

120. "As time goes by," words and music: Henry Hupfield (New York: Harms, 1931).

121. Foucault (1977: 1).

122. John refers to our discussions about the possibility of sending them to the Rössing School in Katatura, the Herero ward of Windhoek. I was able to arrange that in 1981 with the help of Beatrice Sandelowsky, who then was in charge of the school. In addition to John and Damo, Tjitjo also went.

123. Janet Rodney (1980: 93).

References

Achebe, Chinua. 1959. *Things fall apart.* New York: Fawcett.

———. 1977. "An image of Africa: racism in Conrad's *Heart of darkness.*" *Massachusetts Review* 18 : 782 – 94.

———. 1980. "Viewpoint." *Times Literary Supplement,* Feb. 1, 113.

Akhmatova, Anna. 1976. *Requiem and poem without a hero.* Translated by D. M. Thomas. Athens, Ohio: Ohio University Press.

Baines, Thomas. 1968 [1864]. *Explorations in South-West Africa.* London: Longmans, Green.

Beckett, Samuel. 1979. *The Beckett trilogy: Molloy, Malone dies, the unnamable.* London: Pan Books.

Berryman, John. 1956. *Homage to Mistress Bradstreet.* New York: Farrar, Straus and Cudahy.

Bishop, F. 1991. *Polidori: A life.* Chislehurst: Gothic Society.

Böll, Heinrich. 1976a. *Billiards at half-past nine.* Translated by Patrick Bowles. London: Calder and Boyers.

———. 1976b. *Group portrait with lady.* Translated by Leila Vennevitz. Harmondsworth: Penguin.

Borges, Jorge Luis. 1977. *The book of sand.* New York: Dutton.

Britton, Dorothy. 1980. *A haiku journey: Basho's "Narrow road to a far province."* Tokyo: Kodansha International.

Buchanan, Scott. 1975. *Poetry and mathematics.* Chicago: University of Chicago Press.

Byron, George Gordon Noel, Lord. 1933. *The complete poetical works of Byron.* Cambridge: The Riverside Press.

———. 1993. "Dear Doctor, I have read your play." In *Selected poems,* 37 – 40. New York: Dover Thrift Editions.

Cardenal, Ernesto. 1980. "Nicaraguan canto." In *Zero hour and other documentary poems,* 20. New York: New Directions.

Christ, Roland. 1967. "Among the Ibo." Review of *Arrow of god* by Chinua Achebe. *New York Times Book Review,* December 17, 22.

Conrad, Joseph. 1950. *Heart of darkness.* New York: Signet.

Covey, Cyclone. 1961. *La Relación: Adventures in the unknown interior of America.* Albuquerque: University of New Mexico Press.

cummings, e. e. 1938. "MEMORABILIA," from "Is 5." In *The complete poems of e.e. cummings,* unpaged, poem 138. New York: Harcourt, Brace, and World.

Dreschler, Horst. 1980. *Let us die fighting: The struggle of the Herero and Nama against German imperialism (1884–1915).* London: Zed Press.

Durrell, Lawrence. 1962. *The Alexandria quartet.* London: Faber and Faber.

Dürer, Albrecht. 1958. *Niederlandisches Reiseskizzenbuch, 1520–1521.* Basel: Phoebus.

Eliot, T. S. 1952. "The love song of J. Alfred Prufrock" and "Four quartets." In *The complete poems and plays: 1909–1950,* 3–7, 117–48. New York: Harcourt, Brace.

Enzensberger, Hans Magnus. 1968. "Notes to 'summer poem.'" In *Selected poems,* 89. Harmondsworth: Penguin Books.

Ford, Ford Maddox. 1961. *Parade's end.* New York: Alfred Knopf.

Frayling, Christopher. 1991. *Vampyres: Lord Byron to Count Dracula.* London: Faber and Faber.

Freimuth, Gail. 1977. "Girl meets boy." Original manuscript in my possession.

Foucault, Michel. 1977. *Discipline and punish: The birth of the prison.* London: Sheridan.

Grass, Günther. 1976. *Dog years.* Harmondsworth: Penguin Books.

Hardwick, Elizabeth. 1979. "Meeting V. S. Naipaul." *New York Times Book Review,* May 13, 1.

Heinz, Hans-Joachim, and Marshall Lee. 1979. *Namkwa: Life among the Bushmen.* Boston: Houghton Mifflin.

Hindle, Maurice. 1992. Introduction. In Mary Shelley, *Frankenstein, or the modern Prometheus,* edited by Maurice Hindle, i–xxxii. London: Penguin.

Jacoby, Russell. 1975. *Social amnesia: A critique of contemporary psychology from Adler to Laing.* Boston: Beacon Press.

Joseph, M. K. 1964. *Mary Shelley: "Frankenstein or the modern Prometheus."* Oxford: Oxford University Press.

Die Kämpfer der deutschen Truppen in Südwestafrika. 1907. Vol. 1, *Der Feldzug gegen die Hereros.* Berlin: Mittler.

Köhler, Oswin. 1989–97. *Die Welt der Khoé Buschleute.* 3 vols. Berlin: Dietrich Reimer.

LaFarge, Oliver. 1963. *Laughing boy.* Cambridge: Houghton Mifflin.

Leyland, John. 1966. *Adventures in the far interior of South Africa.* Cape Town: Struik. Facsimile reprint of 1866 original published by George Routledge, London.

Long, Haniel. 1975. *The marvelous adventure of Cabeza de Vaca.* London: Picador.

Macdonald, D. L. 1991. *Poor Polidori: A critical biography of the author of "The Vampyre."* Toronto: University of Toronto Press.

Marks, Shula. 1982. Introduction. In S. Marks and R. Rathbone, eds., *Industrialisation and social change in South Africa: African class formation, culture, and consciousness 1870–1930.* London: Longman.

Marlowe, Derek. 1969. *A single summer with L.B.* London: Jonathan Cape.

Marshall, John. 1993. "Filming and learning." In J. Ruby, ed., *The cinema of John Marshall,* 1–134. Chur, Switzerland: Harwood.

Marshall, Lorna. 1976. *The !Kung of Nyae Nyae.* Cambridge: Harvard University Press.

Mead, Margaret. 1979. "Foreword." In Heinz and Lee, xi–xii.

Miner, Earl. 1969. *Japanese poetic diaries.* Berkeley: University of California Press.

Polidori, John. 1819. *The vampyre: A tale.* London: Sherwood, Neely, Jones.

Pynchon, Thomas. 1978. *V.* London: Picador.

Radin, Paul. 1953. *The world of primitive man.* New York: Schuman.

———. 1956. *The trickster: A study in American Indian mythology.* London: Routledge and Kegan Paul.

Rieger, James. 1963. "Dr. Polidori and the genesis of *Frankenstein.*" *Studies in English Literature* 3:461–72.

———. 1967. *The mutiny within: The heresies of Percy Bysshe Shelley.* New York: George Braziller.

Rodney, Janet. 1980. "from Anywoman's lyric." *Montemora* 7:90–96.

Sartre, Jean-Paul. 1964. *Words.* London: Hamish Hamilton.

Seferis, George. 1974. *A poet's journal: Days of 1945–1951.* Cambridge: Harvard University Press.

Shelley, Mary Wollstonecraft. 1974. *Frankenstein, or the modern Prometheus.* Edited by J. Rieger. Indianapolis: Bobbs-Merrill.

Shelley, Percy Bysshe. 1945. *The complete poetical works of Percy Bysshe Shelley.* Edited by T. Hutchinson. London: Oxford University Press.

Shewey, Don. 1986. "Head on knees: David Byrne keeps on making sense." *Boston Phoenix,* Sept. 23, 16.

Snyman, Jan. 1975. *Zhu/ 'hõasi fonologie en woordeboek.* Cape Town: Balkema.

Stevens, Wallace. 1957. "Life on a battleship." In *Opus posthumous: Poems, plays, prose,* 89. New York: Alfred Knopf.

Stocking, M. K. 1968. *The journals of Claire Claremont.* Cambridge: Harvard University Press.

Traill, Anthony. 1994. *A !Xóõ dictionary.* Köln: Rüdiger Köppe.

Webb, Timothy, ed. 1995. *Percy Bysshe Shelley: Prose and poems.* London: Dent.

Willkie, Wendell. 1943. *One world.* New York: Pocket Books.

Williams, William Carlos. 1957. *Kora in hell.* San Fransico: City Lights.

———. 1963. *Paterson.* New York: New Directions.

———. 1967. *I wanted to write a poem: The autobiography of the works of a poet.* Edited by Edith Heal. London: Jonathan Cape.

Wilmsen, Edwin. 1980. "School's out." *Staffrider* 3:31.

———. 1985a. *Killer chill: Poems for the South African peoples' struggle.* Boston: Boston University African Studies Center.

———. 1985b. "Passagen aus 'Journeys with flies—simultaneous biography in the Kalahari.'" *Trickster* 12/13:20–28, translated by Werner Petermann.

———. 1985c. "Return to beginnings." In I. Prattis, ed., *Reflections, the anthropological muse,* 40–41. American Anthropological Association, Special Publication.

———. 1986. "from Journeys with Flies." In Thomas Frick, ed., *The sacred theory of the earth,* 199–219. Berkeley: North Atlantic Press.

———. 1987. "Of paintings and painters in terms of Zhu/ 'hõasi interpretations." In R. Vossen and K. Keuthmann, eds., *Contemporary studies on Khoisan, in honor of Oswin Köhler,* 2:347–72. Hamburg: H. Buske.

———. 1989. *Land filled with flies: A political economy of the Kalahari.* Chicago: University of Chicago Press.

———. 1996. "Premises of power in ethnic politics." In E. Wilmsen and P. McAllister, eds., *The politics of difference: Ethnic premises in a world of power,* 1–23. Chicago: University of Chicago Press.

———. 1997. *The Kalahari ethnography of Siegfried Passarge.* Cologne: Rüdiger Köppe and The Botswana Society.

————. 1999. "Knowledge as the source of progress: The Marshall family testament to the 'Bushmen.'" In K. Tomaselli, ed., *Encounters in the Kalahari. Visual Anthropology Special Issue* 12 : 213–65.

Wissler, Clark. 1938. *The American Indian: An introduction to the anthropology of North America.* New York and London: Oxford University Press.

Yeats, William Butler. 1946. *The collected poems of W. B. Yeats.* New York: Macmillan.